Common Destiny

Common Destiny

Filipino American Generations

Juanita Tamayo Lott

ROWMAN & LITTLEFIELD PUBLISHERS, INC.
Lanham • Boulder • New York • Toronto • Oxford

ROWMAN & LITTLEFIELD PUBLISHERS, INC.

Published in the United States of America
by Rowman & Littlefield Publishers, Inc.
A wholly owned subsidary of The Rowman & Littlefield Publishing Group, Inc.
4501 Forbes Boulevard, Suite 200, Lanham, Maryland 20706
www.rowmanlittlefield.com

PO Box 317
Oxford
OX2 9RU, UK

British Library Cataloguing in Publication Information Available

Library of Congress Cataloging-in-Publication Data

Lott, Juanita Tamayo.
  Common destiny : Filipino American generations / Juanita Tamayo Lott.
    p. cm.
  Includes bibliographical references and index.
  ISBN-13: 978-0-7425-4650-9 (cloth : alk. paper)
  ISBN-10: 0-7425-4650-0 (cloth : alk. paper)
  ISBN-13: 978-0-7425-4651-6 (pbk. : alk. paper)
  ISBN-10: 0-7425-4651-9 (pbk. : alk. paper)
  1. Filipino Americans—History. 2. Filipino Americans—Social conditions. 3.
Filipino Americans—Ethnic identity. 4. Filipino American families. 5. United
States—Emigration and immigration—History. 6. Philippines—Emigration and
immigration—History. 7. Children of immigrants—United States—History. 8.
Immigrants—United States—History. I. Title.
  E184.F4L68 2006
  973'.049921—dc22   2005028527

Printed in the United States of America

♾™ The paper used in this publication meets the minimum requirements of American
National Standard for Information Sciences—Permanence of Paper for Printed Library
Materials, ANSI/NISO Z39.48-1992.

In memory of Patsy Takemoto Mink, Sergio Vieira de Mello, Maximino Lucas Bautista, and Francisco Cachapero.

Contents

Prologue

At a time of major social and economic shifts in the United States and abroad, paradigms of the status quo are not sufficient to explain changing times and future directions. New paradigms are emerging but not yet fully formed (Kuhn 1962). This book is part of the transitional thinking between the old and the new paradigms. As such, it utilizes an eclectic framework that draws from social science, public policy analysis, individual interviews, and participant observation. Furthermore, it is an exploratory rather than a definitive or comprehensive analysis. Hopefully, it will raise questions and generate social science and public policy research agendas for future generations of Filipino and other Americans by younger analysts with a sociological imagination (Mills 1959), a scientific vision of change (Kuhn 1962), and a timeless dream like that of the Reverend Dr. Martin Luther King Jr. Such transitional thinking has begun to occur for other American populations via works such as *A Common Destiny: Blacks and American Society* (Jayne and Williams 1989) and the more recent *Transforming Our Common Destiny: Hispanic Americans* (National Academy of Sciences Panel 2003–2005).

Our initial paradigm for understanding U.S. populations is derived from Western European thought since the 1500s, which placed Western European whites in a dominant position over other populations. The founding settlers of the United States were men of Western science and the Protestant Reformation. They revolted from the "divine right of kings" as manifest by the British and other European monarchies. They wrote the Declaration of Independence and established a representative democracy based on the "self-evident truth" that "all men are created equal." In crafting the Constitution and the Bill of Rights, the American Founding Fathers struggled with a fundamental contradiction between the written word and the real world. All men were not equal. Women were not even recognized in their own right. And because the establishment of the Jamestown colony in the seventeenth century was dependent upon slavery in developing a tobacco-based economy, some men were slave owners and other men were chattel. Slavery as an economic institution of capitalism existed in the United States until the Emancipation Proclamation. In the nineteenth and twentieth centuries, Jim Crow policies, legal cases, and de facto segregation maintained inequality. The foreign policy counterpart of dominance and inequality was known as "Manifest Destiny." First used in 1846 by John O'Sullivan in an article on the annexation of Texas, the concept of Manifest Destiny articulated a popular belief in the United States during the nineteenth century that territorial expansion of the United States was inevitable because of the country's economic and political superiority and rapidly growing population.

One can read U.S. history as a record of the continuing struggles and tensions within this paradox of equality and inequality (P. Foner 1976). The privileged position of the founding settlers continues but is more open to challenge in the twenty-first century. This challenge is due in part to major achievements by the United States in representative democracy and a capitalist economy at home and abroad. At the same time, the American dilemma (Myrdal 1944) of inequality among Americans continues, although it has appeared in different forms over time. The prevailing social order of inequality historically in the United States has been in terms of color (DuBois 1971). The present divide is much more complex, with nuances and implications for the survival of this nation.

As the work of a futurist, this book serves as an alternative framework for understanding the future of the United States, given this country's unique emphasis on the individual and on the rights of the minority when all persons are created equal. This emphasis is juxtaposed with the reality that historically societies do not continue to exist without a strong parent-child bond and the recognition of a higher moral order. I see the Filipino-American experience as an example of the dynamics of individual rights and common group interests. I have written this book as both personal and social narrative to show that, for at least four generations, Filipino Americans have been active civic participants in the United States. They are well-known for being family centered. At the same time, they are all-inclusive because they embrace all sorts of people within their extended families. I think the history of Filipino Americans provides lessons that can be useful in shaping the emerging paradigm of a common destiny for multigenerational Americans in the twenty-first century. This is a common destiny of equality as opposed to a Manifest Destiny that assumes inequality.

A common destiny can be defined on various levels. In the United States it is in the U.S. motto *E pluribus unum*, or, From many, one. Hence, the story of migration of the American pioneers, with the continuing evolution of American-born generations, continues to be a compelling story to tell as each new century brings significant immigration to the United States by immigrants from various nations across the Atlantic, the Pacific, and the Gulf of Mexico. Common destiny can also emanate from shared principles and values. For me, in the twenty-first century a common destiny means something more basic. As British poet W. H. Auden wrote in 1939 on the eve of World War II, "We must love one another or die." For Filipino-American generations, what they continue to contribute toward the common destiny of multigenerational Americans are their renowned skills of caring and hospitality, and the interpersonal skills rooted in their Filipino heritage and nurtured in full civic participation in the United States of America.

Acknowledgments

My work is nurtured by many people in their daily acts of faith, caring, and courage. Along with my immediate and extended family around the world, I owe a debt of gratitude to my many teachers and mentors. These include Willie Mays of the San Francisco Giants; the Daughters of Mary and Joseph who volunteered to follow their Morning Star School students to the U.S. federal government internment camps for Japanese Americans during World War II; the faculty of Mercy High School, San Francisco, including Robert J. O'Neill; all my instructors and faculty advisors at City College of San Francisco; James A. Hirabayashi, Edison Uno, Daniel Feder, and Jovina Navarro of San Francisco State University; Donald J. Bogue, William J. Wilson, Philip M. Hauser, and Mihaly Csikszentmihalyi of the University of Chicago; and Rev. Joseph Guetzloe, Robert Jew, Wray Smith, Bok Lim Kim, Carol Bonosaro, Eugene Mornell, Nampeo McKenney, Peter Bounpane, Wilbur Luna, Robert B. Hill, James Early, Norman Mineta, Margo Anderson, Franklin Odo, C. Matthew Snipp, and Fritz Scheuren. Special thanks are due my children's pediatrician, Pinar Ozand, and their teachers, especially their fourth-grade teacher, Shirley Williams, and principal, Ray Myrtle, Montgomery County Public School System, Maryland.

I also wish to thank my colleagues in the private, academic, nonprofit, and, especially, public sectors. I have used and appreciate the data, research, and analysis of various scholars and practitioners throughout the decades, and particularly that of the stewards of the federal statistical system, the Population Reference Bureau, the Institute for Women's Policy Research, and the Asian and Pacific American Program of the Smithsonian Institution.

This book would not have been possible without four generations of Filipino Americans and post-1965 Filipino immigrants. I am grateful to these interviewees in their 60s, 70s, 80s, and even 90s, and to their younger data gatherers, for their steadfast belief in and support of this project. The interviewees, several of whom actually wrote out in longhand their life stories, were Frederick Velasco Basconcillo, Maximino Lucas Bautista, Rufina Jose Pascual Batara, Consuelo Tecson Begonia, Frank Cachapero, Eusebio Lucas Domingo, Casiana Pascual Lucas, and Anicia Lucas Tamayo. Data gatherers and reviewers included Veronica Tamayo Agustin, Danilo Tecson Begonia, Malcolm Collier, Myrna Lucas Fleming, Daniel Gonzales, James A. Hirabayashi, and Ronald E. Quidachay. I also would like to thank Mitch Allen, and Grace Ebron, formerly of AltaMira Press, and Alan McClare of Rowman & Littlefield for the opportunity they have given me to publish this book. Finally, I thank my husband, Robert Henry, and our sons, David Tamayo and Joseph Henry III, for their unconditional love.

Chapter One

The Future of Nicholas and Fourth-Generation Filipino Americans

The birth of Gregory Tamayo Agustin in February 1972 was a momentous one for our family. It was the birth of my parents' first grandchild. Greg was also the first member of the third American generation of the Lazaro and Anicia Lucas Tamayo family. My brother Bill was so ecstatic about becoming an uncle that he woke me up at 2 a.m. in Chicago, where I was a graduate student, to tell me I was an aunt. I guess I wasn't as ecstatic as he hoped I'd be, but then, he was in San Francisco, a happy undergraduate who didn't think it was ever too late to share good news. I remembered when Billy was born. I'd just come home from kindergarten, and there was a blur of excited relatives and neighbors in front of a crib in my parents' room looking at this tiny bundle. The adults said, "Look, Nita, here is your baby brother, William Robert. He's a boy. He is American born. Isn't that wonderful?" I experienced what passed for sibling rivalry in a five-year-old. I certainly didn't see having a squealing infant who took attention away from me as a good thing. What was so special about being a boy? What was so great about being American born? Since kindergarten, I have asked myself those two questions many times.

I did know by graduate school that Bill and I, along with our older sister, Roni, Greg's mom, were fortunate to have grown up in the United States. We watched our American-born children—Greg, Allan, David, Joseph, Araceli, and Lorenzo (Renzi)—thrive in the same environment. Since the 1950s, Roni, Bill, and I have watched countless relatives and acquaintances leave the Philippines to become U.S. residents and citizens just as my father and uncles did as teenagers and twenty-year-olds in the early twentieth century. But my siblings and I were more than observers of the Americanization experience. We were participants. This was brought home to us at the First Annual Tamayo Family Reunion on Saturday May 7, 2005, in the Filipino Community Center of Solano County in Vallejo, California.

THE TAMAYO FAMILY REUNION, MAY 7, 2005

In summer 2004, I received a call from Roni saying that our Vallejo Tamayo cousins (as opposed to our Vallejo Lucas cousins) wanted to hold a Tamayo family reunion. She had gotten a call from Florie Rumbaoa Barnett. Florie's mom, Felicidad (Belen) Tamayo Rumbaoa, is our first cousin. Our fathers, Lazaro and Venancio, were brothers. To make a long story short, Florie and her sister, Eva Rumbaoa Calilan, had attended their uncle's wife's funeral in southern California several months earlier. Florie and Eva were then reacquainted with their cousins who had immigrated to the United States in the 1990s. Our Philippine-raised relatives wanted to reconnect with their American cousins. We were all excited by the idea of a reunion of four generations of Tamayos. But what a daunting task! Luckily, the Vallejo Tamayo cousins — the Rumbaoas and Thamys — are a well-organized bunch with three generations of U.S. military service, and they are steeped in the burgeoning Filipino-American organizing of Vallejo and the surrounding areas. Not only have the Vallejo Filipino Americans owned their community center for several decades, they are the subject of a book, *Filipinos in Vallejo* (2005), written by Vallejo native Mel Orpilla. In his book Mel documents this Filipino-American community of five generations, starting in 1912 with the pioneer Filipino generation, some of whom went to work at Mare Island Naval Shipyard in northern California. Mel's family and my Vallejo Tamayo cousins fully live the multigenerational reality of Filipino Americans.

At the family reunion, Denny Barnett and Mike Calilan, U.S. veterans and respective spouses of Florie and Eva, kept saying I must get Mel's book. I asked for the publisher, and they said that I could just get it at the local Walgreens. I must admit that I was a bit skeptical about asking for a Filipino-American book at a local drug store. But the Vallejo folks in their live-and-let-live style amazed me. The drugstore clerks and customers — black, white, Hispanic, biracial, Asian — all knew about Mel's book. They were proud that one of their local authors and a pioneer community of Filipino Americans had been recognized.

Our family reunion was a similar moment of pride and recognition. Folks were laid back and just so very happy to meet for the first time or reconnect. Our take-charge cousin, Norma Thamy Bautista, the youngest daughter of my cousin Pete, Belen's brother, organized the e-mail list. By December 2004 she had assigned tasks, and with grace, discipline, and humor she continued to keep everyone in the loop up to the day before the reunion. The northern California contingent served as host of the reunion, which had a Hawaiian theme, because Lahaina, Maui, was my father's port of entry in 1922, and several of his brothers' descendants still live in Kauai and Oahu. Besides, Florie is a veteran Hawaiian-dance instructor. Cousins came from southern California,

Texas, Washington, Maryland, and the Philippines. We ranged from ninety years old to six months old. Our immigrant cousins, children of Felicisimo (Felicing) Tamayo and Ulpiano (Peping) Tamayo Albano, met their multi-generational and multiracial cousins with various ancestries and of various hues, some with southern accents. Showing bemused faces, they slowly absorbed the expansiveness of who is a Filipino American. For those of us who had grown up and played together in the 1950s and 1960s in the Bay Area and then gone our separate ways after graduations and weddings, it was a strange yet happy feeling to see each other as parents and grandparents. We weren't the younger generation. Our children and grandchildren were. We were also fortunate to have two radiant great-grandmas with us: Anicia Lucas Tamayo and Felicidad Thamy. We had so much fun, we decided to hold the Second Annual Tamayo Family Reunion in 2006 in Malibu, this time to be organized by our southern California cousins.

During that first reunion, I kept looking at Norma, all grown up and beautiful who, with my brother Bill, served as mistress and master of ceremonies. The last time I saw Norma she was six years old and the apple of my father's eye. He was her substitute grandpa. When she was two years old in the early 1960s, her dad, my cousin Pete, moved his wife and their five children from Fort Benning, Georgia, to Vallejo to be close to family. Pete was then being reassigned to Vietnam to serve as a U.S. military advisor. Air controllers lost contact with Pete's plane over the Pacific Ocean, and neither the plane nor any of its passengers were ever found. In our multiyear sorrow, we comforted and drew strength from one another. Since then, the Thamys, Rumbaoas, and Tamayos have continued with their lives in the United States. Second and third generations have served in the U.S. armed forces, some even as career soldiers like Filipino-American pioneers Israel Rumbaoa, Pedro Calilan, and Peter Thamy. Others are employed in public service, nonprofit organizations, and the private sector.

I think my dad and cousin Pete would be pleased to see their families thrive, and especially to see their grandchildren and great-grandchildren becoming all that they can be. I have a picture of my dad as a young man in the 1920s standing on the running board of a car with friends. His tie is flying over his shoulder, and he holds a bottle of Coca-Cola. At the family reunion, the Thamy family photo-display prominently showcased an eight-by-eleven-inch photo of cousin Pete standing in front of his huge, white, 1950s convertible. Lazaro and Pete were two young men, two confident individuals with their lives ahead of them. As pioneers and veterans, they understood the importance of the common good. They shared a collective history, were members of communities, and fathered families. At the same time, they were individuals who had dreams and aspirations. They were not afraid to be individuals or to speak up as a minority in the United States, where individual rights and common interests are simultaneously upheld. Such pioneer Filipino Americans as these, including all the Tamayos, Rumbaoas, and Thamys, paved the way for the Filipino-American generations that were to follow.

COMMON DESTINY

I look at five-year-old Nicholas, who is Gregory's first born and Roni's first grandchild. He and seven-year-old Renzi, Bill's son, ran around with the other children at the reunion. Their great-grandparents are Filipino, but their grandparents and parents are Filipino and non-Filipino. Nicholas and his pre-school buddies are part of the digital generation born at the dawn of the twenty-first century. On his Generation-X father's side, Nicholas is a fourth-generation Filipino American; on his mother's side, a fourth-generation Burmese-Chinese American. Nicholas is part of what is popularly viewed as a new phenomenon: a growing multiracial, multicultural U.S. population. In one sense, that represents an achievement of the dream of the late Reverend Dr. Martin Luther King Jr., who believed that children in the United States would be judged by the content of their character rather than by the color of their skin. In a related sense, this fourth generation of Filipino Americans represents coming full circle in the evolution of the settlers of the United States from marginal to mainstream with each successive generation.

The civic values of democracy and equality and a desire for life, liberty, and happiness have been major reasons for the migration of peoples all over the world to the United States since its inception as a colony of Great Britain. The U.S. land mass has grown from that of thirteen colonies of the British Commonwealth to include the vast expanse of the Louisiana Purchase, Spanish America, Russian Alaska, tribal lands of the North American Indians, and a sovereign Hawaiian monarchy. With respect to religion, the European settlers of the United States, beginning with the first Pilgrims and exemplified by the Puritans, emigrated to escape religious persecution and to find freedom of worship. The authors of the U.S. Constitution explicitly recognized in the Bill of Rights the separation of church and state. The outcome of this recognition today is an ecumenical climate in the United States with the reflourishing of ancient religions and the creation of new, more regional, evangelical ones. By contrast, in Western European states with official religions, there has been a sizable decrease in religious participation. In terms of ancestry, we have assumed both pride and shame, as well as ignorance or indifference, depending upon our various circumstances and generations. Our ancestries, communities, and families of origin emanate from the Americas themselves, as well as from across the Pacific and across the Atlantic. Nevertheless, for over two hundred years, U.S. history has depicted American society as a black minority–white majority society, with the rest of society designated as invisible or marginal "Others" (Lott 1993). At the beginning of the twenty-first century, however, we are the first nation-state to recognize officially our multi-ancestral, multiracial, multilingual, and ecumenical reality and to question the utility of racial classifications. This is in contrast to other nation-states that are only beginning to open their borders to immigrants from other nations and cultures, not just as guest workers but as permanent settlers, with great attention to the new, second generation of the twenty-first century. In doing so, they are beginning to establish racial and ethnic classifications for governmental classification.

The popular and the scholarly debates on a future U.S. multiracial and multicultural society assume that persons will be of more than one race or ancestry. There are two points missing from this assumption. First, the land mass occupied by the United States was settled by peoples of various backgrounds and hues before this nation existed. Settlers who preceded British and other European colonists and immigrants were neither black nor white. That is, there have always been different groups with intermingling among them. Second, a multiracial and multicultural mainstream exists today. That is, in various regions of the United States, particularly in metropolitan areas, there exists no dominant race. In large part this is due to immigrants to the United States since 1970 who have come from Africa, Asia, the Caribbean, Eastern Europe, Latin America, and the Middle East. An interesting parallel phenomenon is that Western Europe, with its negative fertility rates, is looking and will continue to look to immigrants from these areas for future population growth.

Today, in major metropolitan areas across the nation there are at least two, and usually four groups with sizable numbers of traditional civil rights populations: blacks, Asians, American Indians, Hispanics, and whites. In selected geographical areas, such as Hawaii and Alaska, American Indians, Alaskan Natives, and Native Hawaiians make up a sizable proportion of the population. All these groups have varying socioeconomic and political resources, leading to the public recognition of diversity within as well as across racial groups. In addition, the multiracial population of the United States is further delineated by interracial and interethnic combinations across groups. Interracial populations are finally being recognized in our post–black-white society almost forty years after the 1967 *Loving v. State of Virginia* Supreme Court case that abolished antimiscegenation laws. As a San Franciscan, I grew up among many racial and ethnic populations. The salient lesson of the 2005 Tamayo family reunion was not only the presence of many races and ethnic populations but also the creation of panethnic (e.g., Filipino Chinese) and interracial populations (e.g., black, white, and Asian).

The traditional civil rights populations and interracial-interethnic populations are joined by the new twenty-first-century Americans of emerging populations from Africa, the Middle East, Eastern Europe, and Latin America who do not fit within traditional U.S. racial, ethnic, or religious groups. Rather than race or color, which derives primarily from the white-black worldview of the Founding Fathers and that was meant to justify inequality between groups (such as suggested in the terms or expressions *chattel*, *three-fifths of other persons*, *inferior dark races*, and *separate but equal*), the new twenty-first-century American suggests the need for a closer look at and contextual understanding of national origins, non-English languages, and non-Protestant creeds. Many of these new settlers are reviving local economies, particularly in the inner cities and in heartland towns with diminishing populations. This phenomenon of various groups coexisting, living, and working alongside one another over decades, with children and grandchildren of every color of the rainbow, is one manifestation of the common destiny of multigenerational Americans. Common destiny, emanating from shared principles and values, reaffirms the connection from one generation to the next. In the twenty-first century, the diversity of U.S. citizens and residents forms a new mainstream that is taking its turn at reshaping U.S. destiny. This new mainstream continues to evolve as the pioneer stock across all ancestries and heritages is replenished by cohorts of new immigrants as well as by multicultural and interracial descendants.

On the other hand, I am concerned for Nicholas and his yet-to-be-born siblings and their generation. I also worry about his dad, Greg, and his uncles— Allan, David, Joseph, and Renzi—and his Auntie Celi. Nicholas's Great-Grandma Anicia, Grandma Roni, and I share a common joy and concern. Our joy is that the first four generations of Tamayos have moved closer to making Dr. King's dream a reality. Our concern is that the American Dream of civic participation and middle-class existence for younger generations may be fading. In 2005, we are finding that providing access and equal opportunity regardless of race and national origin may be necessary but not sufficient for multiple generations of Americans of all colors. The larger social order that allowed earlier generations of the Tamayos, Thamys, Rumbaoas, and other Filipino Americans to thrive is in question in 2005. Just as race and color are no longer only black and white, American families now come in all sizes and composition. My cousins, siblings, and I grew up in a child-centered society as members of the baby boom generation. By the arrival of Generation X, including Greg and Allan, children were a scarce commodity. This was reversed in our families by the births of David and Joseph, who were on the leading edge of the millennial generation, described as the "echo boom," a cohort that outnumbers its parents' generation. In 2005, Nicholas and his digital generation seem to be surrounded by a lot of toys and gadgets, but this does not necessarily mean a child-centered United States today.

This book examines this new, diverse, and complex U.S. population and its destiny through scenes from four generations of Filipino Americans. In doing so, it delineates the ways in which Filipino-American group formation and growth were and continue to be a part of the multigenerational history of the United States. That is, Filipino Americans, like other American populations, are not an absolute group that evolved in a vacuum. Rather, they emerged and grew within a larger context of political forces, a prevailing social order, the established rights and responsibilities of individuals, ongoing economic well-being, and the American Dream. In doing so, Filipino Americans became active civic participants in the American democracy. In 2005, civic participation by Filipino Americans and other Americans is not to be taken for granted.

Nonetheless, active civic participation is crucial, for I believe that the twenty-first century will be defined not so much by the color line as by a more basic human relationship: the adult-child connection, the continuity and change from generation to generation that allow survival of the species. No society survives without sustained commitment and shared sacrifice by men and women for the well-being of younger and future generations. In the twenty-first century, it will take many American towns and cities, as well as a global village, to raise the current and future generations of Filipino-American children and all children.

In the United States, the adult-child connection, as well as a person's relation to his or her fellow humans and to the divine, are strengthened by uniquely American concepts of equality and freedom that range from the Declaration of Independence, the Constitution, and the Bill of Rights to the New Deal and the concept of the Great Society. On the other hand, such human connections have been weakened by salient concepts of inequality and bondage such as implied in the concepts of the Protestant Ethic and Manifest Destiny, and in such expressions as *little brown brother*, and *separate but equal*. Generational connections have, however, been safeguarded by the executive, legislative, and judicial branches of the U.S. government; families and community organizations; public schools and universities; public-health services; and a public safety net across generations for all families. In the twenty-first century, multigenerational Americans have the challenge and opportunity to reaffirm a government of the people, by the people, and for the people, free of intergenerational strife. Their challenges are great.

Chapter 2 focuses on the first, or pioneer, generation of Filipino Americans. This generation was the first to be born under American rule in the Philippines, which almost overnight went from being a Spanish colony for three hundred years to being a U.S. colony. As American nationals, these twenty-year-olds came to maturity in the Roaring Twenties. They claimed their right to a part of the American dream of endless opportunities in the United States just as the American nation-state was poised to become a superpower. As U.S. veterans of World War II, this generation gave birth to the second generation described in chapter 3. These were the children of those pioneers.

The second generation in turn were American citizens by birth or by their naturalization as preschoolers. They were raised in small, sheltered Filipino-American communities, including Oxon Hill, Maryland; Seattle, Washington; and Stockton and San Francisco, California. They were taught to be proud of their Filipino heritage and of their extended families in the United States and the Philippines. At the same time, as residents of segregated neighborhoods and with parents who held occupations that were highly stratified with limited upward mobility, the second generation understood their place as systematically excluded minority Americans. They were taught by their parents, aunts, and uncles how to survive as minority citizens, which included mastery of the English language and of European-based American culture and education. Paradoxically at the same time, their elders nurtured and cherished in this second generation the faith and belief in their power to achieve their dreams in the United States precisely because they had been born or raised in the land of the free.

Before a critical mass of the second generation could rear the third generation, another pioneer generation rose up in the Filipino-American community—the first immigrant generation of Filipinos—the expatriates who arrived in great numbers subsequent to the 1965 amendments to the Immigration and Nationality Act and to the 1972 declaration of martial law by then Philippine president Ferdinand Marcos. Chapter 4 describes and examines this second pioneer generation, the post-1965 immigrant generation, raising more questions than answers. This is a cohort that was born and reared as citizens of the Republic of the Philippines and not as U.S. nationals. They were proud to be Filipino citizens. Upon coming to the United States, they identified themselves as nationals of the Philippines. Nonetheless, like other migrants around the globe who move as human capital with the globalization of the world economy, they made the difficult decision to leave their nation and immigrate to the United States to provide opportunities for their children. They are sometimes conflicted in their allegiances, vacillating from the Philippines to the United States and back again.

All of these prior generations have produced the multicultural and multiracial grandchildren and great-grandchildren that form the focus for the discussion in chapter 5. There is so much yet to know about these third- and fourth-generation Americans with specific ancestry in the Philippines but also from other cultures. It is not clear whether the third and fourth generations of Filipino Americans, or the children and grandchildren of expatriate Filipinos, primarily identify themselves by race, ethnicity, or ancestry. Along with other members of their U.S. cohort, they are beneficiaries of federal civil rights statutes and policies, and of a multicultural and technologically connected global village. In this environment, they can utilize the relatively new choices and freedoms now available to adapt to and take on situational, fluid, and multiple identities as individuals or group members. The final chapter of the book focuses on civic participation in the United States as the third, fourth, and subsequent generations of Filipino Americans move from having been children, followers, and dependents to being adults, leaders, and citizens of the nation-state of the United States of America, and finally to becoming world citizens faced with ensuring future generations in a common destiny.

Chapter Two

Crossing Waters: The Pioneer Generation of Filipino Americans

There is a mysterious cycle in human events. To some generations much is given. Of other generations much is expected. This generation has a rendezvous with destiny.

—President Franklin Delano Roosevelt

Filipino Americans are a truly unique American people because they came to America as U.S. nationals after 1901. This was a bittersweet period in Filipino and Filipino-American history. Nonetheless, Filipinos and Filipino Americans fought for, and continue to fight for, representative democracy. General Emilio Aguinaldo, the first president of the new, independent Philippine nation, despite tremendous odds, successfully led the revolutionary war for independence from Spain. Unfortunately, President Aguinaldo was forced to surrender to the superiority of U.S. military forces and a U.S. government that had allied itself with the Filipinos in their revolution against Spain. The United States quickly replaced Spain as the new colonizer of the Philippines. Hence, Filipinos became U.S. nationals and subsequently Filipino Americans, earning, in my view, the distinction as a truly American people.

The unique status of Filipino Americans compared with other U.S. settlers is related to the fact that Filipino Americans are descendants of Spanish colonizers and Filipino-U.S. nationals. That is, while they are of Asian origin and are part of the Asian-American population, Filipino Americans embody a heritage of both Eastern and Westernized ancestors, language, religion, culture, and worldviews. It is not well-known that Filipino Americans were early migrants to the New World. The early migration across the Pacific of Filipinos to the Americas took place by ship. Between 1565 and 1815, the Manila Galleon trade from Manila to Acapulco was manned by Filipino and Chinese laborers. To escape servile working conditions, it was not uncommon for

11

these laborers to jump ship in Mexico and work their way north and east. The Spanish-speaking Filipinos and Chinese were known as "Manilamen" and are credited with establishing communities along the Pacific and the Gulf of Mexico. The best known are the ten generations of Filipino Americans in what is now the state of Louisiana. According to historian Fred Cordova,

> The first social club founded by Filipinos in the United States has to be the "Sociedad de Beneficencia de los Hispano Filipinas de Nueva Orleans" whose members established in 1870 the Hispano Filipino Benevolent Society of New Orleans and bought a tomb with sixteen vaults in St. Vincent de Paul Cemetery for their burial site. (1983, 2)

The 1910 U.S. Census identified 160 Filipinos. The first three decades of the twentieth century saw 10,000–15,000 young Filipinos, mainly from elite families, arrive in the United States for higher education under government sponsorship as future colonial bureaucrats (Alegado 2002; Posadas 1999, 17). Photos exist of this group, comprised mainly of men, with one or two women, dressed in their Sunday best, exuding self-confidence and pride. Such were the "Jefferson 16," which, according to Cordova, "was the self-given name of this group of Philippine government students, 'pensionados,' who arrived in Seattle on the S.S. *President Jefferson* on September 7, 1925" (1983, 8).

The more popular version of Filipinos crossing the waters, however, is the migration across the Pacific of young, single men from poverty-stricken provinces, many of them teenagers, who heeded the call for workers in Hawaiian plantations, California agricultural fields, and, later, Alaskan canneries. As social worker and Asian American Studies professor Royal Morales wrote in *Makibaka*, one of the first books on Filipino Americans,

> The Sacada program aggressively recruited young, able bodied single Filipinos to work in the sugar and pineapple plantations of Hawaii and in the vegetable and citrus yards of California. The recruits came mostly from the Visayas (southern Philippines) and the Ilocos region (Northern Philippines). (1974, 37)

Pioneer-generation member Maximino Lucas Bautista noted to this author that many young men—teenagers and twenty-year-olds—in his Ilocos Norte province saw going to Hawaii and America as escape from a life of poverty, a way to help their families, a source of potential opportunities, and a great adventure. He was born on November 16, 1913, in Laoag, Ilocos Norte, to Felipe Bautista and Cornelia Lucas, and was the oldest of their eight children. His older cousins Canuto and Eugenio Lucas, who migrated to the United States in the 1920s, advised him to go directly to the mainland instead of Hawaii because plantation work there was much harder than California farm work. Maximino's parents borrowed two hundred dollars for his ship fare.

Because Maximino was a minor, his mother was required to file an affidavit of support allowing him to leave the Philippines and go to the United States. With his cousins and fellow teenagers, Arsenio Lucas Lorenzo and Valerio Lucas, Maximino sailed from Manila on July 3, 1930, for San Francisco; each had a student visa. He noted that while there were many young men eager to travel, there were others who did not want to go to America. They expressed fear of the unknown, fear of discrimination, and reluctance to cross the ocean. There were stories about raging waters, gigantic waves, and of being lost at sea in stormy weather. Moreover, more than one young man had become ill at sea and died. Uncle Max described his ocean crossing with Uncle Arsenio as sixteen-year-olds, each holding back tears as the body of one of their town mates, who had become ill on ship and had died, was placed in a wooden coffin that was wrapped in the American flag, weighted down with heavy iron balls, and then dropped into the vast and deep Pacific Ocean.[1]

PORTRAIT OF THE PIONEER GENERATION

Carlos Bulosan's classic novel *America Is in the Heart* is oftentimes depicted as the portrait of the first generation of Filipinos in America. A complementary view is that Bulosan's portrayal is incomplete, for it begins and ends with a Filipino boy in the promised land, rather than closing with the adult male who would father the next generation. More textured and analytical views of the pioneer generation of Filipino Americans and their offspring were painstakingly created by Royal F. Morales in *Makibaka: The Pilipino Struggle*, and by Ruben R. Alcantara in *Sakada: Filipino Adaptation in Hawaii*. They were further fleshed out in Fred Cordova's visual manuscript *Filipinos, Forgotten Asian Americans: A Pictorial Essay, 1763–circa 1963*. These first portraits have been complemented by more recent works. The Filipino American Experience Research Project, which is housed in the Asian American Studies Department at San Francisco State University and is under the direction of Alex S. Fabros Jr., is in large part based on articles and photographic history from Filipino-American newspapers in Washington, D.C., and the states of Hawaii, Washington, Illinois, and New York. The timeline for this research project is 1898 to 1953. More recently, Janet Alvarado curated the 2003 Smithsonian Institution exhibit Through My Father's Eyes: The Filipino American Photographs of Ricardo Alvarado. Between 1939 and 1959, Ricardo Alvarado took nearly three thousand photos of the San Francisco Filipino-American community and of similar communities in nearby rural areas, recording dances, banquets, baptisms, weddings, funerals, and other gatherings. This archive was not discovered until after his death in 1976 by his daughter, Janet Alvarado. Much of the content of these exploratory studies continues to focus on the post-1898 migrants and, almost as a postscript, their American children.

It is useful to acknowledge that there have been two pioneer generations of Filipino Americans. The focus of this chapter is on the former; the post-1898 migrants, particularly the majority working class. They are also referred to as the Manong generation in Filipino and Asian American Studies and among various generations of Filipino Americans, as well as among Filipinos in the Philippines. The second pioneer generation, the post-1965 immigrants, included many highly educated migrants with characteristics that were similar to those of the Manong generation and their children. Additionally, they exhibited sufficiently salient differences (as will be noted in chapter 4) so as to be classified as another pioneer generation of Filipino Americans. Exploratory and systematic examination of the post-1965 migrants—what I call the expatriate generation—and their offspring is a ripe field for researchers and analysts.

This chapter reaffirms and expands upon exploratory and descriptive research by framing the pioneer generation's story as founding parents of a new population of American children. It is time to update and complete the Manong and Manang generations' stories as established settlers of the United States, and as settlers who achieved permanent residence and citizenship against the odds, thereby ensuring a legacy of Filipino-American children, grandchildren, and great-grandchildren. The initial pioneer generation faced the challenges of the twentieth-century vestiges of Manifest Destiny with their abiding faith in and willingness to work toward a common destiny as they firmly anchored themselves and their descendants in the United States. This is their lasting contribution and legacy.

FROM "LITTLE BROWN BROTHER" TO MANONG

Given that the first generation of Filipinos in the United States was primarily made up of young, single males, the expression *little brown brother* can be viewed as a descriptive, stereotypical term. Its historical connotation, however, is similar to the term *boy* once used to address any black male regardless of age or accomplishment in the rigidly racially stratified black-white social order of the United States (McWilliams 1942). With respect to Filipino-U.S. nationals, *little brown brother* underscored their subordinate status. In particular,

> The Insular Cases gave birth to a new anomalous status, the U.S. "national," a non-citizen, a person who was part of—and even in—America, but not really of it. Like the Chinese, Japanese and others ineligible to naturalization, the "national" could not vote, serve on juries, acquire land, form corporations, or work at those professions that required United States citizenship as a prerequisite. As a result,

the Filipino "national" similar to other non-whites, came to be confined to the residential areas and occupational niches that their alien status and widespread color prejudice in America consigned them. Their children born on US soil were American citizens but all too often were made to bear the stigma attached to their racial ancestry and other legally defined "color." (Alegado 2002, 5)

Their agricultural work under the hot sun in Hawaii and California made their brown skins darker. Yet rather than being "little brothers," as defined by the American social order, in their familial roles they were oftentimes the oldest children of a Filipino family, the ones who were most able to work like a man. They were the *manong*.

Manong is the Ilocano word for older, or big, brother; *manang* means "older sister." These terms are honorifics, a sign of respect, particularly when used for the eldest sibling who served as surrogate parent. *Ading* means younger sibling and is gender neutral. In traditional Filipino society, persons are not addressed by their given name alone. Rather, a name is preceded by the appropriate honorific denoting relationship such as *Manang* Biday or *Uncle* Sebio. The personal names themselves are usually abbreviated versions or nicknames. The members of the Manong generation sat at my family's dinner table regularly during the 1950s before Tuesday night wrestling matches or after weekend baseball games. They often babysat for my siblings and me. We children did not call them *manong* because they were not our older brothers. If we were directly related, then we called them *uncle*. If we were not directly related, we addressed them as *tata*, the Ilocano word for "father" with the feminine version being *nana*, meaning "mother." We addressed the elderly as *lolo* or *lola*, meaning "grandfather" and "grandmother," respectively.

In some respects, the Manong generation has been romanticized as a low-income, poorly educated group of bachelors, like the bachelor society of the Chinese in nineteenth-century America. It is true that many had hard lives, faced daily discrimination, and lived their last decades in poverty (Takaki 1989, chap. 9; Scharlin and Villanueva 1992). As sociologist Antonio Pido noted,

Almost all Pilipino immigrants to the United States across time have had to face racial discrimination and prejudice in one form or another. However, the early immigrants were at a disadvantage due to their low socioeconomic backgrounds and lack of educational and professional credentials and to the fact that they were immigrating to the U.S. at a time when racism was more overt and virulent. (Pido 1985, 123)[2]

On the other hand, the Manong generation did not die out. They wooed and married the Manangs. They became husbands and fathers. They became U.S. soldiers and citizens. They owned homes and businesses. They organized Filipino organizations and labor unions They provided the infrastructure of business and government services while working behind the scenes as blue- and pink-collar workers in the apartment, hotel, and food industries, and as accountants, clerks, and postal workers in the private and government sectors.

A few left wives and sweethearts in the Philippines when they migrated to the United States. The vast majority of Manongs who gave up bachelorhood for Filipina maidens, however, did so not as youths but as seasoned adults in middle and old age. They took brides who were a generation or so younger than they were. This was due in large part to their inability to support a family on migrant, low-income wages and to restrictive naturalization, miscegenation, and immigration policies discouraging the formation of Filipino families in the United States. Not until immigration and naturalization policies were relaxed during World War II were pioneer-generation Filipinos able to return to the Philippines to marry. Not surprisingly, they married younger women of child-bearing age. According to my mother, Anicia Lucas Tamayo, my father and uncles looked for strong women who had survived a hard childhood and who were willing to work with stamina to withstand economic and social discrimination in a new land. Still other pioneer-generation Filipinos met and married Filipino women who had migrated separately on their own to the United States after World War II.

Like the Chinese and Eastern European immigrants before them who had intended to come to the United States only as temporary laborers to make enough money and return to their homelands, the Manongs found themselves putting off their return for a variety of reasons (Morales 1974, 51–58; Scharlin and Villanueva 1992, 24). Before long, they had spent most of their lives in America. Those who served in World War II and were stationed in the Philippines came to the strategic conclusion that the future was in the United States. Despite its imperfections, the United States held political and economic opportunities particularly when compared with a war-devastated Philippines. The pioneer generation could best support their relatives and compatriots by being a voice for Filipino concerns in the United States and by remitting dollars to the Philippines. The tradition and pattern continue today via Filipino overseas workers and immigrants to the United States and other nations. The bulk of these pioneer-generation members returned to America as their home, bringing their Philippine-born wives to Hawaii, Seattle, San Francisco, Los Angeles, and the agricultural fields of Stockton and Delano, California. They bore American children; they sent remittances to help relatives in the Philippines; and they sponsored relatives as immigrants to and permanent residents in the United States.

THE GREATEST GENERATION COHORT

The pioneer generation born under American rule were part of the U.S. generation demographically termed "the greatest generation." They are credited as the Americans who lived through the Depression, fought World War II, and contributed to unprecedented postwar peace and posterity. In Sonny Izon's film *An Untold Triumph: The Story of the 1st and 2nd Filipino Infantry Regiments of the U.S. Army*, second-generation Filipino Americans born in Hawaii and California marveled at the superior strength, stamina, and performance of the pioneers, many of whom were in their late thirties, forties, and even fifties during World War II. In military exercises and full combat, the Manong generation proved to be as competitive as, or more so than the Hawaiian and West Coast–born younger generation who had not endured similar hardships. The presence of the "greatest generation" on center stage coincided with the dominance of American global leadership in the twentieth century. All things were possible. The sky was the limit.

Man-Child of the Roaring Twenties

Looking at photos of my father, Lazaro Lorenzo Tamayo, and his friends in his album of this period, I see confident, even cocky, handsome, young men. They fit in easily in a new culture based on the self-evident truth that all men are created equal. In the United States, they could be self-made men unbounded by the hierarchy of the Catholic faith or the stratified society of Spanish colonizers. Educated in the English language in an American-run public-school system but also familiar with the colonial, Spanish life of their elders, they learned early in their lives that they could strive to be individuals and not just members of ascribed groups. The photos in the Ricardo Alvarado exhibit and Cordova's book, as well as in the hundreds of photo albums of pioneering Filipino-American families, uniformly show seemingly immortal men-children in their zoot suits or three-piece pinstripe suits with matching handkerchiefs and ties and pomade-styled hairdos on their way to taxi-dance halls. The photos also depict young men with their worldly possessions, the new inventions of early twentieth-century America: sewing machines, radios, phonograph players, cameras, and automobiles. I particularly like the photo mentioned above, of a few of these young men with feet planted on the running board of a 1920s convertible, hands holding bottles of Coca-Cola, and neck ties blowing in the wind of the California countryside.

Like Janet Alvarado, I stumbled upon one of my dad's treasured possessions many years after he died in 1978. It was a small—four-by-six-inch—black, six-ring binder with eclectic contents: various names, addresses, phone numbers; quotes from politicians, including Abraham Lincoln; Spanish vocabulary words; notes on his plumbing jobs; a list of his favorite English- and Spanish-language phonograph records; and speeches to various Filipino organizations in the United States. The one speech that intrigued me the most was from

November 16, 1939, a presentation to the Philippine Aviation Club of America. My dad was an honorary aviator. He had wanted to be a barnstormer. Since 1920, his goal had been to be a pilot; however, it was not a goal he would reach. He wrote, "It has been my ambition 19 years before to be an aviator but was unable to do because of the high price of an hour of the course so I put it aside but not morally." My dad goes on to honor the members of the club, particularly a Mr. Esteban, who was the instructor and technical adviser of the group of aviators. My dad praised them for their perseverance to be pilots at great sacrifice. He then went on to speak about President Lincoln's many business and political failures before his successes, noting that Filipinos in the United States would also face many more struggles as well as opportunities, particularly on the eve of World War II. It is hard to say how many aviators were present, but my dad noted that the size of his audience was about fifty people.

When I think of my dad and his friends, many of them were risk-takers who envisioned a world of countless opportunities and individual freedom. Like other American pioneers before them, they faced a rugged, often solitary life in the vast, diverse, virgin, and untamed lands of California, Hawaii, Washington, and Alaska. Like the western cowboys, trappers, and farmhands before them, they spent a great deal of their youth and early adult lives without the civilizing effects of women and children. They faced the rule of the frontier. They had to be self-sufficient with a strong sense of survival. While low wages and discrimination were certainly a daily part of their lives, they also saw economic and political opportunities that were not available in the Philippines. Even as a U.S. possession or as a commonwealth, the Philippines was governed for the foreseeable future not only by Americans but also by a controlling oligarchy of mestizo landowners from a legacy defined by Spanish colonization and the entrepreneurial acumen of Filipino-Chinese businessmen.

Sweet Sixteen or Seventeen in the Depressing Thirties

For a long time the pioneer generation of Filipino Americans was defined by the Manongs, not the Manangs. The photos of young Filipinos on the West Coast in the 1920s include young, white, Mexican, and on occasion, American-Indian and black women. Filipino females of any age are noted for their absence. Official statistics bear out this imbalance in Filipino sex ratios. Louis Bloch, a statistician for the California Department of Industrial Relations, wrote,

> Out of every 100 Filipinos who came to California during the ten years 1920–1929, 93 were males and 7 were females. During the 10 years considered there were admitted to California 1,395 Filipino males for every 100 Filipino females admitted. While the ratio of Filipino males to females coming to California is 14 to1, the ratio of males to females in the total California population is 1.1 to 1. Among the female Filipino arrivals the proportion married is twice as great

as among the male Filipino arrivals. About 43 per cent of the Filipino females coming to California are married women, whereas only 21 per cent of the Filipino males coming to California are married men. Only about 12 per cent of the married Filipinos bring their wives with them upon coming to California. There are more single persons and less married persons among the Filipino arrivals into California than among immigrant alien Mexicans, or among immigrant aliens, exclusive of Mexicans admitted into the United States. (Bloch 1930, 11–12)

Based on an interview with Veronica Tamayo Agustin on March 14, 2002, Rufina Jose Pascual Batara (also known as Ruth or my Nana Pinang) entered the United States for permanent residence on December 30, 1930. She was seventeen years old, arriving in San Francisco during the Depression. She came to the United States at the prompting of an older married sister, Juana, even though their mother protested. Each weekday morning, she took the bus to Galileo High School near Fisherman's Wharf, mainly to learn English. There were a few Filipino and many Chinese students. Ruth had been born April 5, 1913, to Jose Jose and Demetria Quines Jose in Piddig, Ilocos Norte. She was delivered by a midwife at home. She was the fourth of eight children, and her father was a salesman and businessman in Cagayan who had gone to work in Hawaii with her two older sisters, Juana and Josepha. As a child, Ruth played shortstop in the children's baseball games. She carried water in a jar, cared for younger siblings, and pounded rice. Her favorite subject was geography because she liked learning about other places; she also learned to play the harp from an old man who taught music. In San Francisco, she worked as a waitress in a Filipino restaurant, the Rizal Café on Kearny Street, for five days a week for about a year. Many Filipino male customers of the restaurant tried to befriend her; there were very few Filipino women. She met her husband, Epitacio "Pete" Pascual, through her brother-in-law, Manuel Mariano, who was Pete's uncle. She says, "At first, I was scared of him and tried to hide when he came to visit my sister and brother-in-law. I thought he came to visit them but later I found out I was the one he wanted to see. He worked in a drugstore, bringing me gifts of candies, soap or perfume when he called on me. We went to shows and family picnics." Eventually Pete and Rufina married and began raising a family. During World War II, she and Pete worked across the bay in Richmond in a shipyard burning metal for shipbuilding while their children went to a babysitter in San Francisco. She says life was very hard but happy. She and her husband were one of the first Filipino families to buy a home in the Richmond District ("the avenues") of San Francisco in 1954. Her aspirations for her children, Betty, Reggie, and Linda, were that they finish their education, support themselves, and be independent. She was widowed after thirty-two years of marriage. Ruth also outlived her second spouse, of thirteen years, Telesforo Batara, and her son. She is proud of being able to take care of her home and premises, enjoy her friends, and still attend parties. When I visited her in May 2004, she still possessed, at ninety-one years old, the carriage, grace, intelligence, and beauty of Queen Rufina I, Miss Filipino American of 1933.

Another young Filipino American of this time, Maximino Lucas Bautista, turned sixteen in 1930. He worked in Stockton, California, picking grapes for five to ten cents an hour under President Herbert Hoover's administration during the Great Depression. By 1932, under the administration of President Franklin Roosevelt, wages were raised to twenty cents an hour. Uncle Max noted that,

> When I could make one dollar a day, I felt rich. In the summer time I worked in the fields with Arsenio from 5 a.m. to 5 p.m. Then we would get picked up by our boss to go back to town to our hotel to shower and eat dinner. We would go to night school from 7:30 to 11:30 p.m. After a while, we quit school. We also worked in the canneries in Ketchikan and Kodiak, Alaska.[3]

From Nationals and Scapegoats to Union Organizers and Americans

Following the carefree spirit of the Roaring Twenties, the Great Depression of 1929 was a difficult coming-of-age for the pioneer generation. This decade challenged all Americans as distinctions and inequalities between citizens and aliens hardened. More and more, Filipino-U.S. nationals and other imported laborers were targeted as competition for white labor and were accused of taking jobs from white men. According to California government statistician Louis Bloch,

> The Filipinos have also replaced white workers in other occupations. In box factories at Weed, Susanville, and Westwood, for instance, the Filipinos are hired extensively in places formerly held by white men. According to "Organized Labor" of May 12, 1928, the official organ of the California Building Trades Council, the Filipinos in San Francisco "are forcing their way into the building industry, many of them working as engineers, painters, electricians, carpenters' helpers, and laborers."
>
> In agricultural occupations, the Filipinos largely compete with Mexicans, Chinese, Japanese, Hindus, Portuguese, Porto [*sic*] Ricans, Koreans, Turks, and other foreign born groups. But even in some of these occupations Filipinos are taking the place of white workers. Many tasks in fruit picking, such as peaches, apricots and cherries, formerly done by white labor, are now being done by Filipinos. This is also true in harvesting rice, in picking hops, and in general ranch labor. The exact extent to which Filipinos have displaced white labor can not be readily established, but it is not unreasonable to suppose that, with the increase of Filipinos in the state, further substitution of Filipino labor for white and other labor will take place. (Bloch 1930, 72–73)

In reporting on an anti-Filipino riot in Exeter, California, on October 24, 1929, Bloch concluded that,

There is no doubt that this outbreak against Filipino was due primarily to the racial feeling of antagonism developed among the white laborers against the Filipino laborers who were displacing them in harvesting the Kadota figs and Emperor grapes in and about Exeter. (74)

With respect to the more commonly known Watsonville riot on January 21–23, 1930, Bloch concluded,

The immediate cause of the Watsonville riot was the employment of white female entertainers by the Palm Beach Filipino Club at Watsonville. The details of the affray were already reported in California newspapers and therefore need not be described here. It is important, however, to point out that although the use of white girls as entertainers was the immediate cause of the riots, the real cause of the Watsonville riot was the unwelcome influx of Filipino labor in Monterey County. (Bloch 1930, 74)

In the 1930s, the treatment of blacks and foreigners, including Filipino-U.S. nationals, was consistent with nineteenth-century periods of nativism. According to Susan Evangelista,

Racism and economic pressures combined to give rise to vigilantism, groups of white men rounding up and expelling "foreign" workers from various farming towns. Actually the history of such actions against Filipinos goes back to the 19 September 1928 expulsion of Filipino workers from Yakima Valley, Washington. But as the thirties wore on, expulsion became a more common method of eliminating unwelcome labor competition. Filipino workers all over the coast, forced to take drastic wage cuts because there were simply no other jobs available, were accused of bringing wage levels down; yet if they went on strike they were herded into makeshift jails, or shot outright, and accused of trying to overstep their own racial "limitations." (Evangelista 1985, 4)

As they had done earlier in the 1920s in Hawaii under leaders such as Pablo Manlapit (Alcantara 1981, 27–28), Filipino-U.S. nationals on the mainland organized into labor unions and went on strike.

Perhaps the most characteristic response of the Filipino community to the hardships they encountered was to participate in labor organizations and to form unions. This they had to do for themselves, as the existent American labor organizations of the time—notably the American Federation of Labor—were simply not interested in organizing farm workers or in dealing with "alien" workers. Early unions such as the Filipino Workers Association attempted to affiliate with the AFL but were rebuffed, but later did join the Trade Union Unity League

and then the Cannery and Agricultural Workers Industrial Union. (Evangelista
1985, 6)

Under such divisive conditions, the pioneer generation displayed resilience
and perseverance. Moreover, they understood and lived a common destiny
with other laborers.

> Filipinos quickly demonstrated a rather mature attitude toward supporting the
> strikes of workers of other ethnic groups, joining with white lettuce packers in
> Salinas in 1936 and later with Mexican grape pickers. (And much later, Filipino
> workers actually started the great Grape Strike of 1965 generally attributed to
> the Chicano labor leader Cezar [*sic*] Chavez). They showed again and again that
> they understood the importance of refusing to underbid for labor contracts or
> break the strikes of other groups. (Evangelista 1985, 6–7)

Of this difficult period, Carlos Bulosan would be inspired to say through his
characters in *America Is in the Heart*,

> We in America understand the many imperfections of democracy and the malignant
> disease corroding its very heart. We must be united in the effort to make an Amer-
> ica in which our people can find happiness. It is a great wrong that anyone in Amer-
> ica, whether he be brown or white, should be illiterate or hungry or miserable.
>
> We must live in an America where there is freedom for all regardless of color,
> station and beliefs. Great Americans worked with unselfish devotion toward one
> goal, that is, to use the power of the myriad of peoples in the service of Amer-
> ica's freedom. They made it their guiding principle. In this we are the same; we
> must also fight for an America where a man should be given unconditional op-
> portunities to cultivate his potentialities and to restore him to his rightful dignity.
>
> It is but fair to say that America is not a land of one race or one class of men.
> We are all Americans that have toiled and suffered and known oppression and
> defeat, from the first Indian that offered peace in Manhattan to the last Filipino
> pea pickers. America is not bound by geographical latitudes. America is not
> merely a land or an institution. America is in the hearts of men that died for free-
> dom; it is also in the eyes of men that are building a new world . . .
>
> America is the nameless foreigner, the homeless refugee, the hungry boy
> begging for a job and the black body dangling on a tree. America is the illiter-
> ate immigrant who is ashamed that the world of books and intellectual opportu-
> nities is closed to him. We are all that nameless foreigner, that homeless refugee,
> that hungry boy, that illiterate immigrant, and lynched black body. All of us, from
> the first Adams to the last Filipino, native born or alien, educated or illiterate—
> We are America! (Bulosan 1943, 188–89)

The ability to find common ground despite the economic polarization of the
Depression served the pioneer generation well as preparation for the fascism
that was spreading across Europe and the imperialism of Japan that resulted
in World War II.

Citizen Soldiers

Like the Navajo code talkers of World War II, who fought not just for the United States but for their ancestral lands and communities in the Southwest, Filipinos in the United States and Hawaii (which was still a territory) actively sought to fight in World War II to liberate the Philippines from Japanese occupation. Unfortunately, as they had been classified as "aliens ineligible for citizenship," they were also ineligible to join the U.S. armed forces. Linda Revilla noted that this did not stop them.

> Shocked by the bombing of Pearl Harbor and the Japanese invasion of the Philippines, the Filipino American community petitioned President Franklin D. Roosevelt for the right to fight. Their first of several victories arrived in 1942 when the law was changed to allow Filipinos to join the service. (Revilla 2003, 1)

Similarly, Alex Fabros Jr. reported on this historical moment,

> Mass meetings of Filipino organizations were held in various cities approving petitions and resolutions asking President Franklin D. Roosevelt to allow the more than 135,000 Filipinos in the states to join the U.S. Armed Forces. They also approved resolutions about the feasibility of organizing a combat Filipino battalion. (Fabros 1994, 1)

Then, in 1942,

> On 8 April before Bataan fell to the enemy, the Filipino Infantry Battalion was activated at Camp San Luis Obispo. Lieutenant Colonel Robert H. Offley, a brilliant West Point graduate who had several tours of duties in the islands and spoke an understandable Tagalog and the son of the last military governor of the island of Mindoro, was named as its commanding officer. There were only three enlisted men and seven officers when the unit was activated. And of course, jubilation and unfathomable joys gripped all the continental Filipinos about the activation. (Fabros 1994, 1)

According to veterans featured in Sonny Izon's documentary film *An Untold Triumph: The Story of the 1st and 2nd Filipino Infantry Regiments, U.S. Army*, becoming American soldiers in World War II was for these men their rite of passage from youth to manhood.

Recognition of Filipinos as part of a more inclusive America, not just as "little brown brother," was further affirmed when Carlos Bulosan was recommended to write an article, "Freedom from Want," that appeared in the March 6, 1943, edition of the *Saturday Evening Post*.

> In 1943, when the war had finally lifted the United States out of the Depression, the *Saturday Evening Post* published four articles on the four freedoms—Freedom

of Speech, Freedom to Worship, Freedom from Want, Freedom from Fear—and ran them in a special issue with Norman Rockwell illustrations. It was decided that "Freedom from Want" should be done by someone who had really known physical want, and Louis Adamic recommended Bulosan to the *Post* editors. (Evangelista 1985, 15)

This change of attitude was also reflected in federal policies. According to Revilla,

The valor of the men of the 1st and 2nd Filipino Infantry Regiments and that of Filipino soldiers in the Philippines who fought and died side-by-side with the Americans helped change the American attitude toward Filipinos for the better. One result was the 1946 change in the law that allowed Filipinos in the United States to be eligible for naturalized citizenship. Regiment members brought "war brides" back to the United States, and their families transformed Filipino American communities. The veterans took advantage of the G.I. Bill of Rights, went to college, and became business and community leaders. The 1st and 2nd Filipino Infantry Regiments were the catalyst for change in the post-war Filipino American community. As one veteran eloquently declares, "serving in the Regiments was our emancipation." (Revilla 2003, 3)

As the child of a World War II veteran, I attended a few meetings of the Veterans of Foreign Wars (VFW) with my dad in Alameda, California, in the 1950s. He and my uncles and their mainly Filipino friends would wear VFW hats and conduct formal meetings in the living room as I ran around and played hide-and-go-seek with the other children of veterans. It was just something else to do in my childhood, like watching my dad and the other Filipino dads go out one evening a month to meetings of the union of apartment, hotel, and restaurant workers. I was also aware that several of my cousins, on both the Tamayo and Lucas sides, had chosen military careers, mainly in the army, navy, and later the air force. California was full of military bases. Filipino-American communities grew around such camps as Hunter's Point and the Presidio in San Francisco, Mare Island near Vallejo, and Camp Pendleton. Navy towns such as San Diego, Virginia Beach, and Norfolk also became focal points for establishing thriving, multigenerational Filipino-American communities.

Husbands and Wives, Fathers and Mothers, Uncles and Aunts

The works of Alex Fabros Jr. and Sonny Izon honored our fathers, mothers, aunts, and uncles collectively and publicly. They also helped me understand and appreciate the personal stories of such individuals, including the story of my family's next-door neighbor Francisco Cachapero, who died in October

2005 at the age of ninety-three. I call him Cayong Frank. *Cayong* is the Ilocano word for "brother-in-law." The beauty of languages with various relational honorifics, such as Ilocano and other Filipino dialects, is that when using them one can automatically describe how one is related to others in any social context, including the various types of in-law contexts. While Cayong Frank is not really my brother-in-law, he was married to a distant niece of my dad and so respect and common courtesy dictated a formal address. He was also a pivotal person in my family's ability to own a home in 1958. As I mentioned earlier, Ruth and Pete Pascual's ownership of a home in "the avenues" of the Richmond District in 1954 was a significant accomplishment both for them and for the Filipino community. After all, it was not until 1968 that housing segregation by race was abolished by federal law. While San Francisco was not a city of the South, there were definitely areas that were off-limits, both de facto and de jure, to nonwhites—areas such as Forest Hills, Pacific Heights, and Sea Cliff. While Filipino Americans were excluded as residents of these tony neighborhoods, they were present there in day jobs as janitors, houseboys, and other domestic help.

What intrigued me about Cayong Frank was that with his charm, competence, and confidence he was able to buy a home in upper Haight Ashbury, which was then a completely white-resident neighborhood. At least in "the avenues," a few Chinese and Japanese homeowners had preceded the Filipino ones. Cayong learned that his next-door neighbors, the Irish Catholic Kellys, were ready to retire and willing to sell their home directly without a real-estate agent serving as middleman. Despite an initial hesitation, and encouraged by Cayong, the Kellys sold their home to my parents, immediately doubling the number of Filipino families in the neighborhood. It was only decades later that I understood Cayong Frank's ability to persuade and deliver. In 2002 and 2003 when I was interviewing him for this book, he modestly acknowledged that he was one of a few men from the World War II Filipino regiments rigorously chosen to train in intelligence. Frank Cachapero served with General Douglas MacArthur in Australia in planning and executing the invasion of the Philippines, which was under Japanese rule. He chose to be a paratrooper rather than join the submarine invasion forces. It was a dangerous mission that he had never considered even in his wildest dreams. It was also a major life experience that he spoke of later with gusto and the smile of a fun-loving boy even at ninety years old.[4] He was instrumental in the liberation of the Philippines and in helping at least two Filipino-American families to own their own homes.

The individual stories of the wives, mothers, and aunts of the pioneer generation are less well-known. Although sex ratios nationally for Filipinos in the United States had fallen from 10:1 in 1910 to 5:1 in 1940, by 1950 females comprised just over one fourth (27 percent) of the Filipino-American population (Urban Associates 1974, table B-5).

The young Ruth Batara, attending high school in San Francisco, working in the shipyards, and being a homemaker to the second generation of Filipino Americans, represents the prewar pioneer-generation women. Consuelo Tecson Begonia, a World War II bride of a Filipino American, represents wartime pioneer-generation women. She was interviewed for this book in spring 2002 by her only child, Danilo (Dan) Tecson Begonia, currently professor of Filipino and Asian American Studies, as well as former dean of the School of Ethnic Studies, San Francisco State University. Born in 1914 in San Miguel, Bulacan, Consuelo had parents named Luis Tecson and Filomena David. Her father was part Spanish-Chinese, very educated, very strict. He had been a law-school classmate of Manuel Quezon (president of the Philippine Commonwealth), but left his studies to serve as a captain for the Philippine Army during the Filipino-American War. After the war, Consuelo and her eight siblings were brought up and strictly disciplined in the Spanish tradition. Active in school and folk dances, she mainly played and studied because her house was run by housekeepers. She attended the Catholic convent school of La Consolacion College, where she trained as a seamstress and beautician with European teachers—Spanish, Swiss, and Dutch. To help support her younger siblings, she ran a dress shop and beauty parlor for more than ten years after finishing high school, and she met her husband during World War II.

> I married my husband, a total stranger. Never dated, never kissed, never go out, never went to a dance. He was a fast worker. He was in the army. It was an accident that I married him. A total stranger. He was a soldier assigned to my place. He belonged to the underground. He fell in love with me. In wartime the marriages are fast, no waiting, so he married me because he was going back to the states. I was married October 5, 1945, and lived in Camp Turlock, General MacArthur's headquarters for the 978th Signal Corps, before moving to the states.[5]

Consuelo noted that even though coming to the United States was a difficult adjustment, she was very satisfied with her life. She worked much of her married life outside the home, including in farm fields. Yet, she managed to travel to sixteen countries in Europe and to send her son to college and Europe. She was proud of her son, daughter-in-law, and grandchildren.

My Uncle Arsenio Lucas Lorenzo in his forties married Auntie Corrine, then a nineteen-year-old Mexican American. He gave up working in the Alaskan canneries and instead raised five children with her in Porterville, California, where he was a foreman in the vineyards. Every fall he sent my family a crate of seedless Thompson grapes via Greyhound Bus. In the summer of 1958, my family was visiting his. I and my siblings and our cousins picked clumps of grapes all afternoon, eating them to our hearts' delight until we got sick. Uncle Max Lucas Bautista also married later in life, at fifty-two, to Auntie Ludy, a nurse from La Union who immigrated to the United States in 1965. They raised their sons in Carson, California, in the outer Los Angeles suburbs. They were a two-income family of shift workers, a situation prevalent among Filipino Americans and other minorities in the 1950s and 1960s, particularly because Filipino Americans and minorities were disproportionately employed in lower-paying service industries such as restaurants and hotels.

My mother's older brothers, on the other hand, returned to the Philippines in the 1930s. My Uncle Eugenio returned to his wife, Restituta, in the Philippines. He joined the Philippine Constabulary, and she taught elementary school in Laoag, Ilocos Norte, where their two children were born and raised. His brother, Uncle Canuto, went back to the Philippines (after living with his older white common-law wife, Grace, in California) to marry a Filipina. Their matrimony was brief because Canuto contracted pneumonia a few weeks after their marriage. It is said that his mother and siblings attributed Uncle Canuto's illness to the complete baptismal immersion he underwent when converting to his bride's religion.

My father Lazaro provides yet another picture of these Manongs who became husbands and fathers. He went to the Philippines to marry Canuto and Eugenio's younger sister, Anicia, in 1940. He returned to San Francisco early in 1941 without his wife because her mother, my Lola Basalisa Paguirigan, did not want her daughter to deliver her first child in the United States with no one to assist her. Then World War II intervened. Like many couples separated by the Pacific Ocean, my parents had no communication during the war years. According to my mother, she and my infant sister spent a lot of time on the run going from one hiding place to another—from her granduncle's farm in the interior to the mountains with the Philippine guerrillas—to escape the Japanese military. For his part, my dad participated in civil-defense practices on the West Coast, including citizen patrols during blackouts in San Francisco. When the U.S. government decided that Filipino nationals in the United States could join the armed services, he joined the U.S. Army in California as part of the Filipino regiment. He became one of the first Filipino Americans in World War II to become a U.S. citizen in 1943 when Filipino-American soldiers were allowed a brief window of opportunity (a few months) to become naturalized citizens.

In 1946 after the war, my parents and sister were reunited in the Philippines. I was born a few years later, but my dad returned to the United States to work, leaving my mom, my older sister, and me in Laoag. This pattern of working in one nation while one's family remains in the homeland is similar to the work patterns of Asian and other immigrants who came before and after my father. It continues today as overseas Filipinos and workers from other poor countries migrate to richer nations for the work that will help them feed their families back home. Bringing his family to the United States was uppermost in my father's mind. This was poignantly brought to my attention while I was going through old family papers in 2003 with my sister. Here is an unedited excerpt from a February 19, 1951, letter from Lazaro Lorenzo Tamayo to Anicia Lucas Tamayo:

> Now Aning even my application by the State and Immigration Depts. had approved we only are one third ahead yet of the result. And the work is plenty more. The best way to do is that you have to obtain all those certificates which may costs
>
> Birth certificates all 6 copies @ 1.30 pesos = 7.80 pesos
>
> Marriage certificates 2 copies @ 1.30 = 2.60
>
> Police record certificate 2 copies @ 1.00
>
> Total 12.40
>
> Plus your passport pictures 9 copies
>
> We have to do and acquire all three *biagco*[6] and send them to the American Embassy Consular Section via registered mail. If we don't do this action we might as well forget your coming to the States. But I am more positive that you come. You see what happened of Korea. The Communist forces ran over by was twice and the U.N. are forwarding north for the 2nd time. According of the world's prophecy now all the small nations will be over run by machines of war. And they even predicted if a third world war comes may last from 15 to 20 years. They figure that way because of the almost balance strength of the powerful countries. And what to you think darling, we might as well do it now *biagco*. I will hear what you say dear. I got a letter from Arsenio today. He said he went to work in San Pedro since Nov. and just returned to Porterville last week. That is why we didn't know where he was. I will write more *biagco* and my love and kisses to three of you . . . Your daddy, Lazaro

This personal letter is not just about my parents. It also depicts the administrative detail, long-term framework, and world geopolitics that many members of the pioneer generation considered in their calculus to leave the Philippines and become Americans. Like other American pioneers before them, the first generation of Filipino Americans had a sense that they were going to new and unknown environments that would be perhaps harsh but were also promising. They were willing and courageous risk-takers bent on improving their destiny and that of their children.

The personal stories of the struggles and sorrows, the hopes and dreams of these young and middle-aged men and young women reveal a generation who wanted to live to become husbands and wives and fathers and mothers. They chose to be parents and doting aunts and uncles of children born and raised in the United States as American citizens. They chose to be godparents. My brother Bill's godparents include the San Francisco Filipino Americans Bill Fonacier Sr. of the Philippine Consulate, hotel and apartment union officer Pablo Placido, and physician Elvira Lao, one of the first female Filipina doctors in the United States. What their stories also reveal are persons with assets—the typical migrant social capital—confident enough to leave their homeland for a strange land, and bringing with them a steady vision or dream for a better future and the willingness to make great sacrifices and to work and persevere under tremendous pressure. In addition, as products of the American educational and legal system, they possessed additional survival skills: a command of written and oral English, familiarity with the U.S. Constitution and American history, and the ability and perseverance needed to navigate the U.S. social order, including its bureaucracies.

MIGRANT SOCIAL CAPITAL MEETS THE AMERICAN SOCIAL ORDER AND ECONOMIC WELL-BEING

The majority of the pioneer generation were working-class immigrants with limited formal education. Yet they were able to lay a foundation that would allow their children to become part of the American middle class. These two generations were then positioned to participate in an expanding U.S. economy. With much of Europe and Asia devastated by the war, the United States was in a unique position to grow with little competition from other nations. Furthermore, the GI Bill for returning World War II veterans allowed working-class Americans entry to the middle class through free higher education, preferences in hiring, and low-interest home mortgages.

These first- and second-generation Filipino Americans became part of an American social order that emphasized individual freedom and equality in the post–World War II era. In 1947, Jackie Robinson would break the color barrier in that quintessentially American sport, baseball. No longer now were some of the best U.S. baseball players relegated to segregated teams, most notably the Negro League. This was not just a historical note for Filipino Americans. A major feature of the pioneer generation of the Filipino Americans and their children, and one that distinguishes them from the third and fourth generations and post-1965 immigrants, is that the former lived and worked in a racially segregated America that had been the norm historically despite the Civil War and passage of the Thirteenth, Fourteenth, and Fifteenth amendments to the Constitution. With the Emancipation Proclamation of 1863 and the defeat of the slave states' secession from the Union, slavery in the United States had been abolished. Nevertheless, almost immediately after Reconstruction, racial resegregation occurred, manifested in Jim Crow policies and court decisions that continued to support white supremacy. The court case with the greatest impact on blacks and other U.S. racial minorities after the end of slavery was *Plessy v. Ferguson*, the 1896 landmark Supreme Court decision that established the policy of "separate but equal" in public facilities for whites and blacks.

Early Filipino Americans identified with the struggles of black Americans to break the color barriers—not only the struggle of Jackie Robinson but also those of Joe Louis, Paul Robeson, Philip Randolph, Nat King Cole, Marian Anderson, and Jesse Owens. Their children's heroes included Willie Mays, Roberto Clemente, Martin Luther King Jr., and Malcolm X. In school they identified with black Americans whose contributions were documented in U.S. history books: Crispus Attucks, Frederick Douglass, Harriet Tubman, George Washington Carver, Booker T. Washington, and W. E. B. DuBois.

The removal of the color barrier in sports was followed in education by the landmark 1954 *Brown v. Board of Education* Supreme Court decision outlawing segregated education. Through this landmark decision, the nineteenth- and early twentieth-century form of Manifest Destiny—as reflected in the Jim Crow era of "separate but equal"—was eliminated in education. On the fiftieth anniversary (1954–2004) of this historic unanimous decision of the Supreme Court justices, it is useful to remember that *Brown v. Board of Education* served as the catalyst for breaking down legal barriers in public service, employment, housing, and other segregated areas of American life for the twentieth and twenty-first centuries. The paradox of the postwar era was that although the emphasis at the time was on Americans' common destiny, this was also the period of the House Un-American Activities Committee investigations, driven by Senator Joe McCarthy's twentieth-century version of the Salem witch trials. In 2004, the paradox is playing out again. While there continue to be many programs for remembrance of, reflection on, and appreciation of the *Brown* decision, the civil liberties and rights of American citizens, prisoners, and visitors are being limited during the U.S. war on terrorism and as a result of American combat in Afghanistan and Iraq.

Along with structural economic and political opportunities, the social capital of these early Filipino Americans served them well in surviving and thriving in the United States. In explaining the strength of immigrants new to the United States in the twenty-first century, current immigration researchers note that

> Social capital is distinct from human capital in that it does not presuppose formal education or skills acquired through organized instruction. Instead it originates from shared feelings of social belonging, trust, and reciprocity. The concentration of immigrants of various nationalities in particular niches of the labor market occurs via word-of-mouth recommendations. Those in turn, are made possible by immigrants' memberships in social networks whose members vouch for one another. (Kelly 1996, 34)

In addition to social capital as it relates to labor-force opportunities, Alcantara described the social capital inherent in the fundamental Philippine cultural importance attached to smooth interpersonal relationships in his study of the pioneer generation in Kenhale Plantation in Oahu, Hawaii.

> The first challenge of social living on the plantation town, therefore, consisted of instituting some kind of order among the Filipinos in the camp. In the barrio, this was done automatically through the extended family. Its elders, whether male or female, imposed discipline on the members. Barrio people knew each other and it was enough merely to remember that bad behavior brought shame not just to the self but to the extended family. The ideal relationships were those among kinsmen; a kinsman never betrayed you, always assisted you in times of need or trouble, accepted you without question, supported you in your aspirations, and provided social allies. Strangers were always brought into a kinlike relationship.
>
> This same strategy could be used in the camps. Respecting age differences within the extended family led to widespread usage of such terms of address as *manong* (older brother or kinsman) and *tata* (elder) among the Kanhale Filipinos; thus they became known to others as [*sic*] *manongs*, with the stress placed incorrectly on the second syllable. The same strategy could also be used among the single males assigned to a communal household; they could create a sibling order based on age, with everyone deferring to the eldest and most mature for the organization of household tasks and settlement of disputes. This sibling order, operating out of mutual consent among its members, was a fragile one though; it worked best usually when the members were actually kinsmen or came from the same home town.
>
> The other Kenhale groups also heard the Filipinos address each other as *bayao* (brother in law) and *pare*. Being a *compadre* (shortened to *pare*), a co-parent sponsor at the baptism or wedding of a child, formally established kinlike relationships between the parents of the child and the sponsor, and thus created the necessary obligation of mutual assistance, trust, and respect. (Alcantara 1981, 56–57)

Another aspect of social capital relates to solidarity based on common adversity. In his extensive work on late twentieth-century and early twenty-first-century immigrants to the United States and their children, sociologist Alejandro Portes identified two elements that were also found in the Filipino pioneer generation:

> A common cultural memory brought from the home country and which comprises the customs, mores, and language through which immigrants define themselves and communicate with others . . .
>
> An emergent sentiment of "we-ness" prompted by the experience of being lumped together, defined in derogatory terms, and subjected to the same discrimination by the host society. (Portes 1995, 256)

THE ROOTS OF CIVIC PARTICIPATION
AND SOCIAL ORGANIZING

Two factors—growing up as U.S. nationals and being able to adapt Filipino social capital to an American setting—were instrumental in the pioneer generation's adjustment to permanent settlement in the United States. For example, as U.S. nationals, they participated as students in social and civic clubs like 4-H, and in various oratorical societies and debating clubs. In addition, their religious upbringing also contributed to the formation of civic participation and organizing. Their Spanish legacy, as it was rooted in Catholicism, was structured hierarchically, with the religious at the top and the laity below. Such a background was useful when one was participating in the hierarchical order of military life both in the Philippines and the United States. In addition, the altruism and voluntarism inherent to Catholicism provided a familiar and effective infrastructure that could be used for organizing the early and later Filipino-American generations. As youths in the Philippines, the pioneer generation headed religious organizations, such as the Organization of the Sacred Heart and Legion of Mary in Laoag, Ilocos Norte. They grew up in a culture that prized service to God and others. Like to Italian and Irish Catholics, they came from families that encouraged their children to become priests, brothers, or nuns and to do good works. Major life events were noted in the church through the formal and sometimes elaborate rites and rituals of christenings, weddings, and funerals, as well as through the social festivities that attended them. Catholic Filipino Americans honored their dead on All Saints' Day and All Souls' Day with masses and novenas. My siblings and I remember kneeling through wakes and nine-day novenas for the dead, during which all the prior generations of the immediate and extended family were individually named, along with the litany of the saints and mysteries of the rosary.

Fred Cordova lectures across the nation on Filipino-American history to both Filipino-American audiences (such as chapters of the Filipino American National Historical Society) and the general public (such as the National Museum of American History in Washington, D.C.), and he often states that whenever two *Pinoys* (a name initially used internally among Filipino Americans) got together, they formed a club. When a third Pinoy joined them, they organized themselves into a Filipino organization. The pioneer generation was certainly known for its plethora of social organizations, ranging from provincial or even municipal identities such as the Laoaguenos to fraternal organizations such as the Caballeros de Dimas Alang, which was a Philippine organization that established its first American lodge in 1920 in San Francisco (Cordova 1983, 180). The charter of the Filipino Community of Seattle, formed as early as 1926, combines appreciation for Philippine heritage with civic participation in the United States.

"Community," according to Filipino American organizers having to resolve mutual needs in yesteryears, traditionally has meant a formal organization in a particular locality of members of Filipino ancestry and their spouses, governed by a charter, authorizing duly elected officers, to achieve specific objectives by performing such tasks as "to promote and protect the interests of Filipinos; to cultivate unity and cooperation among all Filipinos; to foster and establish better relations and sympathetic understanding between Filipinos and non-Filipinos; to encourage a unified observance of Philippine events of national or historical importance; to provide members with facilities for wholesome recreational, social, educational and cultural activities; to foster and instill civic spirit and cultural pride among Filipinos; to coordinate with the city, county, state and national officials in all matters affecting the welfare of Filipinos" (from the Charter of the Filipino Community of Seattle). (Cordova 1983, 175)

By 1940, social organizing had moved to the next level of civic participation. Going through my parents' boxed photographs, I came across eight-by-eleven-inch black-and-white studio photographs of the International Family Circle. The earliest photo is dated April 19, 1942, and is titled "Third Anniversary and Grand Ball in Honor of the Installation of Officers of the International Family Circle." It shows two Filipinas in full-length evening gowns with corsages holding bouquets of assorted flowers; four Filipinos in tuxedos, one with a white bow tie; and three Filipinos in custom-tailored suits with breast-pocket handkerchiefs. They are young or middle aged, good looking, and confident as they raise their right hands, standing on some stage. One of the women is Mrs. Buted. The other is a woman I called Nana Tasing, who with her beauty shop was one of the first Filipina business owners in San Francisco. One of the men is my Tata Puri, a young Telesforo Batara who eventually married Rufina Pascual. The other man I recognize is my father. Another photo, undated, shows a young Filipina in a strapless light evening gown with a huge bow and sash falling from the left side of her waist. The head table below includes another young woman, Carol Mariano, niece of Rufina Pascual, in a high-collar gown with a sash that reads, "Miss International Family Circle." Also seated are two adult Filipinas. One is Mrs. Mata, with the big butterfly sleeves that were associated with Filipino fashion at the time. The other seated guest is a white woman wearing a white hat. The table is decorated with ferns, carnations, other flowers, and a banner that reads, "International Family Circle 1940." Each word is on a different line. In the middle of the banner between *Family* and *Circle* is a drawing of the globe. In a wider photo of the head table, I discover the identity of the white woman in the hat. She is the wife of George Christopher, who was later mayor of San Francisco. They are the only two non-Filipinos at the head table. There is also a white middle-aged woman in uniform, serving the dinner guests. The photo caption reads,

"Photo above was taken during the installation and inauguration of officers for 1951–1952 of the International Family Circle of San Francisco, Calif. Installed by president Board of Supervisors, S.F. Mr. George Christopher. Held at the Mart Club, San Francisco, April 21, 1951, Photo by Manuel Nery."

The pioneer generation was also versed in using the legal system. For a long time, I had assumed that legal housing segregation by race and national origin had been eliminated by the 1968 Civil Rights Act. Certainly one of the first things our parents taught my siblings and me even before we started school was knowing the different racial and ethnic neighborhoods in San Francisco and their boundaries. We initially lived in a flat in Japantown, which was the buffer zone between the blacks of Fillmore and the whites of Pacific Heights. It was only by looking at old family pictures, with my college friends Anita Sanchez and Joe Alfafara, that I learned about the California Supreme court case *Alfafara v. Fross* (1945) 26C2d358. Celestino Alfafara, Joe's uncle, successfully challenged the California 1921 Alien Land Act, which prohibited aliens not eligible for citizenship from owning property. In June 1944, Mr. Alfafara had entered into a contract to purchase land in San Mateo for sixty-five dollars. Bernice Fross, the owner of the land, refused to convey the property, citing the Alien Land Act. The court ruled that Celestino Alfafara was not an alien but a U.S. national who owed allegiance solely to the United States and not to a foreign government (the Philippines was then a commonwealth). *Alfafara* was another step forward in greater civic participation and equality for Filipino Americans specifically, and in general for other Americans, paving the way for other steps that culminated in Title VIII of the Civil Rights Act of 1968, also known as the Fair Housing Act.

Union Organizing

The history of Filipino-American union organizing commonly focuses on the 1920s and 1930s when the Manong generation of plantation and farm workers established unions to fight for rights such as equal pay for equal work, and again in 1964 when Filipino farm workers under the leadership of Larry Itliong and Philip Vera Cruz began a sit-down strike in the Coachella, California, vineyards. That strike launched what was to become the United Farm Workers Union, under the leadership of Cesar Chavez, and a national boycott of California grapes. What is less known is that after World War II, Filipino Americans expanded union work to major metropolitan areas when they formed families and permanent communities and entered the urban labor force. The war opened up higher-status occupations, which had been traditionally reserved for white men, to people of color, as well as to white women, as symbolized by Rosie the Riveter. When veterans returned from the war, white women and people of color were expected to again support a white-male breadwinner economy. Filipino Americans used unions to publicize and correct employment issues such as fair labor standards, a living wage, occupational segregation by race and gender, retirement pensions, and survivor and other benefits.

Key Infrastructure Service Jobs

Throughout their history in the United States, Filipino-American men and women have maintained high labor-force participation rates. There are several reasons for this. One is the strong work ethic of the Filipino people. Among the majority poor, earned income is a necessity for survival. In addition, in pre-Hispanic Philippine societies, women held legal and economic power in their own right. This value has persisted even in the postcolonial era, with Filipino women controlling the purse strings in families and with girls encouraged to seek higher education and professions. Another reason for this strong work ethic is specifically that Filipinos were initially and continue to be recruited as workers for the U.S. economy. Furthermore, Filipinos in the United States, even as they have entered the middle class, are still a source of income for their family members in the Philippines. Promoted and encouraged by former Philippine President Ferdinand Marcos in the 1970s, overseas domestic workers continue to be the Philippines' greatest export and revenue source. Having more than one job per person, or having more workers per household compared with other American households, is a characteristic of Filipino-American households. Most of our mothers worked to help our fathers support their families. Certainly for decades, as low-wage earners, many families combined full- and part-time jobs. Even when they were able to retire from the military or civilian work forces with pensions and union retiree benefits, Filipino-American men and women did not necessarily leave the paid labor force.

In addition to having high labor-force participation rates, Filipino Americans positioned themselves in key infrastructure service jobs. Union membership taught them the importance of standing up collectively for worker rights, including steady, preferably permanent, jobs, with benefits such as defined pensions, life insurance, and health insurance. The contributions of the Filipino-American Army regiments in World War II, coupled with integration of the armed services by President Harry Truman after World War II, opened up career opportunities in all branches of the military to Filipino Americans and other people of color. In addition, the United States has a long-standing policy of recruiting Filipinos in the Philippines for the U.S. Navy (Quinsaat 1976).

On the civilian side, Filipinas began to be recruited as nurses in the United States (Choy 2003). Also, retired veterans took the infrastructure skills that they had developed in the armed services into the civilian world as administrative and clerical staff, technical workers, postal employees, and workers in a range of hospitality-related positions. Like blacks, who kept and continue to keep the

White House infrastructure running, Filipino Americans were exposed to the power elite of San Francisco, Los Angeles, Seattle, and even Washington, D.C. They served as White House stewards. With strong representation in the Restaurant, Hotel and Apartment Building Union, they served as waiters, cooks, busboys, and janitors in first-class hotels and Pacific Heights residences. They learned from their employers how to carry and conduct themselves among the upper class and how to participate in upper-class matters such as investment, sophisticated legal rights, and college educations for their children if not for themselves. Filipinos also began small businesses specific to serving the growing Filipino-American community. They established businesses that included barber shops, beauty shops, grocery stores, restaurants, and professional services (such as are provided by tax accountants, lawyers, and physicians). This pattern was and is similar to that of other minority groups that were not readily accepted by mainstream businesses as employees or clients.

THE SUCCESS OF THE PIONEER GENERATION

The pioneer generation left the Philippines as U.S. nationals and single young men, many in their teenage years, to find opportunities for employment, education, and adventure. They thought their migration was temporary. For a few it was, but for the vast majority, U.S. migration turned into permanent residency. This first generation not only had to make a living for themselves, but they also were often expected to be a source of income for their impoverished families in the Philippines. They were initially relegated to the lowest-paid occupations, becoming farm workers and other manual laborers, and were therefore subject to discrimination on the basis of color, race, and citizenship. Despite social, political, and economic discrimination, however, this pioneer generation succeeded as citizen soldiers, active civic participants, and as a critical labor force in an industrial United States. Equally important, these prolific old-timers established Filipino-American families and communities, ensuring multiple generations of Filipino Americans.

Success was partly due to a post–World War II shift in an American society that had defended democratic institutions abroad by defeating Fascism, Nazism, Japanese imperialism, and the ideology of the supremacy of an Aryan race. Among other changes, this societal shift opened traditionally white-male jobs to people of color and white women. Nonwhite Americans, such as the American Indians and Asian Americans who fought in World War II, were finally allowed to become naturalized citizens in 1952. There was no looking back. The people of the United States became more receptive to freedom and equality at home in the post–World War II era. That is, the emphasis was on a common destiny. While reaffirming their Filipino heritage, the pioneer generation of husbands and wives, mothers and daughters, and aunts and uncles envisioned the United States as the future for themselves and their children. Their sons and daughters and nieces and nephews were not to be Filipino-U.S. nationals but fully participating American citizens of Filipino ancestry.

NOTES

1. Maximino Lucas Bautista, interview with the author, March 3, 2002. Mr. Bautista (my Uncle Max) died in December 2004.

2. Since the late 1960s, the Filipino community in general and scholars in particular have debated the use of *Filipino* or *Pilipino*. Most writers use *Filipino* and some *Pilipino*. Pido provides a background statement that encompasses most of the reasons for *Pilipino*. "The Philippines was named *Las Islas Filipinas* (Philippine Islands) after Felipe (Philip) II of Spain (1527–1598). Spaniards born in the Philippines of pure Spanish parentage were called *Españoles Filipinos* or *Filipinos* for short, to distinguish themselves from the Spaniards born in Spain who were *Españoles Peninsulares* or simply *peninsulares*. Those of mixed (native and foreign) parentage were referred to as *mestizos* and those with mixed Spanish blood, specifically were *creollos*. When the United States took over the country from Spain, the name of the country was Anglicized to the Philippines, and all the native born were called Filipinos. None of the seven major Philippine linguistic groups have an 'f' sound. The people refer to their country as *Pilipinas* and themselves as *Pilipinos*" (Pido 1997, 37).

3. Maximino Lucas Bautista, telephone interview with the author, March 3, 2002.

4. I never formally interviewed Cayong Frank. He was interested in my book and would tell me snippets of stories but we didn't get a chance for an oral interview. The closest we got was mid-March 2002 when he and I were at Kaiser Hospital in San Francisco, in my mom's room, and he told me stories while we waited for my mom to awaken. He had taken a couple of hours off from constant care of his wife, disabled for several years.

5. Dan Begonia, "Mom's Interview," transcript of videotaped interview, 30 April 2002.

6. *Biagco* is a word of endearment used for sweethearts, spouses, and one's children. Its literal translation is "my life."

Chapter Three

The Dinner Table:
Children of the Pioneers

There are two lasting gifts we can give our children. One is roots and the other is wings.

— Traditional folk saying

It takes a village to raise a child.

— African folk saying

In the 1950s and 1960s, as Filipino-American families joined the vast American middle class and became urban homeowners, they looked for good-sized houses. This was necessary not only to accommodate parents and several children, as the offspring of prolific Filipino-Catholic families, but also to house the assorted relatives and friends who might be visiting for weeks from the Philippines, or passing through for several days during the rotation into and out of migrant seasonal work from the rich California San Joaquin Valley to Kodiak, Alaska, or who might be just looking for temporary residence between jobs. In particular, our pioneer-generation parents looked for houses with big dining rooms. Fortunately, they were not difficult to find in places like San Francisco, with older homes from the Victorian era when families and guests were entertained at home. My cousins and I spent countless hours sitting at dinner tables laden with a huge variety of Filipino and American dishes made from the freshest produce and seafood of California's fields and waters. We learned firsthand how to discriminatingly eat (but not always prepare) good food, as well as how to practice the high art of Filipino hospitality. Several of our fathers were chefs and head pantry men at some of the finest Bay Area restaurants and hotels, retired U.S. Navy cooks, and assorted San Francisco restaurant dishwashers and bartenders. We were taught how to serve and socialize with all kinds of guests, from sophisticated Spanish and

American mestizos, Philippine government officials, Philippine businessmen, and very bright but shy Filipino seminarians from the provinces on their way to the Vatican for graduate studies, to fresh-off-the-boat, non-English-speaking immigrants from the barrios. As the cousins ran around chasing each other after meals, the adults lingered at the dinner table mixing English, Ilocano, Tagalog, and even Spanish, resorting to deep Ilocano when they didn't want us to understand what they were saying. They told stories and jokes; caught up on gossip; shared job tips; debated over whom to vote for in local politics and in the perennial Filipino-community queen contests; commiserated over problems with relatives; and relived good wrestling matches at Winterland while reanalyzing past duels between the San Francisco Giants and the Los Angeles Dodgers.

THE SECOND-GENERATION FILIPINO AMERICANS

A prerequisite for examining the tensions between Manifest Destiny and common destiny in relation to the children of the pioneers is an understanding of the contextual use of the term *second generation*. In this book, *second generation* refers primarily to the children of the pioneer generation described in chapter 2. This use is distinct from that of current immigration researchers and popular media portrayals of immigrants, such as the 2003 movie *Bend It Like Beckham* in its portrayal of a pioneer- and second-generation Pakistani family in Great Britain. In his extensive immigration research, Alejandro Portes (1996, ix–x) identified post-1965 cohorts as "second generation." His use of the term, adopted by current immigration researchers, "includes native-born children of immigrant parents and children born abroad who came at a very early age, sometimes called the 1.5 generation" (Rumbaut and Ima 1988). Differences in the use of *second generation* have to do with a base time period and the nationality of immigrants. The children of immigrants described by current researchers refer to children of the post-1965 period, especially those born after 1980, whose parents immigrated from non–Western European nations, namely from Asia, Latin America, the Middle East, and Africa. Portes calls them "the new second generation" (1996), in contrast to the sizable second generation produced by nineteenth-century European immigrants from across the Atlantic who arrived during and subsequent to the Industrial Revolution in the United States.

This broad brush categorization omits the small but crucial U.S. migrations of people of color in the early half of the twentieth century, namely the transnational migrations of Filipinos and other Asians to the West, Mexicans to the Southwest, and Puerto Ricans to the Northeast. These movements mirror the internal migration of blacks from the rural South to the urban Northeast and Midwest. This is a crucial point because it was this initial pioneer generation and their U.S.-born children who called the United States their home. For most of these, life in the United States was their frame of reference. Steeped in American culture and heritage, they defined themselves as Americans and defended their rights and responsibilities as U.S. citizens. They were the children of color, born and raised in the United States, who continued in the 1960s and 1970s to break the color barriers of Manifest Destiny that their parents and ancestors had confronted and begun to remove from the founding of this nation through the 1950s. I call this cohort the *new second generation*—the children of nonwhite, Anglo-Saxon Protestants whose parents also settled in the United States and whose fathers served in wars undertaken by the United States, even when they were not allowed to be full citizens.

This distinguishes them from post–World War II and post–civil rights Philippine expatriates and their children, who may be ambivalent about being primarily American or who are unclear as to what being an American means in terms of the U.S. Constitution, U.S. history, and the U.S. legal system. These expatriates and their children are the subject of chapter 4. This chapter will focus on the children of the pioneer generation. These children can be divided into two generations as defined by demographers and social commentators: the silent generation, and the baby boom generation (Strauss and Howe 1991).

The Silent Generation

The silent generation roughly encompasses persons born before the Depression through the end of World War II. This was a relatively small cohort, particularly compared to the baby boomers who followed them. Asian-American autobiographies and biographies of this generation include *Fifth Chinese Daughter* by Jade Snow Wong, *Woman Warrior* by Maxine Hong Kingston, and *Rice Room* by Ben Fong-Torres. With respect to Filipino Americans of this period, Bob Santos's memoir *Hum Bows, Not Hot Dogs* weaves his personal history into the larger story of the Asian-American community and its movement and power structure. The strength of this autobiography is its multidimensionality in addressing the cyclical issues of an individual growing up and of the political development of the Seattle Filipino- and Asian-American communities. Santos describes his multicultural family, including his American-Indian grandmother and the death of his young, beautiful mestiza mother shortly after his birth. He and his brother, Sam, were raised by their extended family of grandparents, aunts, uncles, and by their father, lightweight boxer Sammy Santos, who lived like many of the bachelor Manongs in a hotel in the International District of Seattle. The Santos brothers were involved in various close-knit Filipino-American community events, social gatherings, and sports. They served in the U.S. armed forces, married early, raised many children, and joined the American middle class of the post–World War II era, including the labor-force entry into the Boeing company. In the late 1960s, Bob returned to the International District, providing leadership in organizing the Filipino- and Asian-American communities and helping them to work systematically and strategically with municipal, county, state, and federal agencies. He led in the revitalization of the International District, a wonderful textbook study of the age-old story of David and Goliath, and in this case one in which developers threatened to evict retired Manongs and other low-income, single elderly from their residence hotels to make room for a stadium and other commercial establishments.

Another member of the silent generation whose personal history can also be viewed as an example of what other Filipino Americans experienced after World War II but before the civil rights movement of the 1950s and 1960s is Fred Basconcillo. The following is an unedited transcript taken from Mr. Basconcillo's unpublished autobiography.

My name is Frederick Velasco Basconcillo. I was born on April 11, 1937, at 154 Russ Street an apartment in the south-of-Market area of San Francisco to Artemio Espiritu Basconcillo and Maria De La Cruz Velasco.

My parents immigrated to the United States from Villasas, Pangasinan, P.I. in the 1920s. I had an older sister, Elizabeth, dob 2/14/32-dod 1986, and older brother, Benjamin, dob 7/16/31-dod 2000. My father was born 1901 died 1981. My mother was born 1902 died in 1988. During the 1930s until World War II, my parents had a business at 826 Kearny Street between Jackson and Pacific Streets. It was called the New Luneta Café. Next door was Tino's Barber Shop. It was on the same block as the International Hotel, 848 Kearny Street. It was a typical Filipino business for that area. There was a three-chair barber shop in front, immediately behind that was a pool hall, and at the back of the pool hall was the café where my mother did the cooking. I didn't find out until many years later that behind the café was my father's main business, he ran a huge gambling hall. His clientele included the movers and shakers of San Francisco's politics and high society. One of his patrons was the notorious Sally Sanford who had the same clientele as my father. I guess every once in a while my parents would bring me to the gambeling hall because I've seen pictures of me when I was about three or four years old in the arms of some of his patrons while they visited the establishment.

My earliest recollections of that time were not very good. I guess it was the summer before I started kindergarten when my parents boarded me in a Convent somewhere in the North Beach area. I think it was also on Kearny Street. There were other kids there too. My parents would come and visit me every day, sometimes twice in the same day. But, the part I hated the most was Friday afternoons, the parents of all the other kids would come and take them home for the weekend, my parents would come and visit as usual but leave me there, as I found out later, would go back to work. I hated being the only child at that Convent on weekends. My sister and bother were at a summer camp called Hill Farm somewhere in San Mateo.

From Russ Street we moved to a flat on Minna Street then to another flat at 642 Natoma Street, all in the south-of-Market area. Then, some time around 1939 or 1949, we moved to the Fillmore (Western Addition). First to a flat on Ellis Street than to flat at 1728 Sutter Street between Laguna and Buchanan Streets. I attended kindergarten through second-grade at Raphael Weil Grammar School. Then my mother transferred me to Morning Star Catholic school. After graduating from Morning Star, I took the entrance examination to Saint Ignatius High School, I passed but was not admitted. All my other white friends were, even the ones with lower scores than mine. My mother enrolled me in Sacred Heart High School instead. This was not my choice! I changed, I became rebellious. During my freshman year I got into trouble and was expelled. I completed my high school studies at Galileo High School.

Growing up brown (as a Filipino) in San Francisco had many angry memories for me. From an early age, I was very independent. I didn't want to depend on my parents for money to buy toys or other things that I wanted. I wanted to be able to earn my own money. The first job I got when I was about eight or nine years old was delivering the *Call Bulletin* newspaper. I remember one instance when I asked my supervisor if he would assign me to one of the big apartment buildings in the Marina district, and he did. When I went to introduce myself to the building manager, I got a big surprise. He didn't want ME in the building, he wanted an "American boy"! I couldn't understand what he mean. I guess that's when the anger started building up inside me because that was the first time I had experienced that feeling, but it wouldn't be the last.

As a teenager growing up in the Fillmore, I found there were other Filipino kids suffering the same bad experiences. There was a large Filipino community in that area. In fact, The first Filipino Community Inc. of San Francisco was founded there and the first Filipino Community Center was opened on Geary Street between Laguna and Octavia Streets. My mother enrolled my sister, brother, and me into the Filipino Children's club founded in 1936. And when we got older we were members of the Filipino Teen club sponsored by the Filipino Community, Inc. I am still a life member. I remember the fund raising events they used to raise money for the organization. Queen Contests were a favorite form of event. my sister had her share of participating these contests (reluctantly). They would have the Social Box dances. The girls would prepare a box (often times a handkerchief) and the men would bid on the box, the bidder would bid, or put, an amount of money, and would dance with the girl until somebody put a higher bid then the higher bidder would cut in an dance with the girl and this would go on until there were no more bids. The highest bidder would get the box.

There were other ways of raising money for the organization. My father was a member of the Legionarios Del Trabajo (a Filipino Fraternal Organization). Often time they would rent a hall (California Hall on Polk Street) and they would sponsor Taxi Dances where the men would purchase tickets, ten cents apiece, approach a woman, many women were invited by the organization (mostly non-Filipino), give her the ticket and dance with her for one dance. One ticket, one dance. At the end of the evening, the women would turn in their tickets and the organization would pay them half of what they collected. Many organizations did this. The Caballeros De Dimaslang and the Grand Oriente, just to name a few.

As a teenager, in addition to high school sports, I got involved in organized sports with a Filipino team named the San Francisco Mango Athletic club, founded in 1939. They were involved in an organized league that participated in various sports, such as softball, basketball, volleyball and football, we completed against other Filipino teams throughout California. The Mangos also sponsored a girls' basketball team named the Mangoettes. My future wife was a Mangoette. She was born and raised in Berkeley and attended San Francisco City College.

I graduated from high school in 1954 and married Patricia Anderson (white father, Filipino mother) in 1956, We had four children. When we first married, we lived with my parents at 1370 Gilman Avenue in the Bayview district. I was working as an Iron Worker, my wife was working as a nurse. After a couple of years we saved enough for a down payment on a house. We bought our first house not far from my parents home in the Bayview, it was a fixer upper. It was not exactly what we wanted but it was what we could afford at the time. We put a lot of work into the house and after two years we were able to sell it at a good profit and look for something we really wanted. It was some time in the late 50's or early 60's when we found what we thought we wanted, but we faced something that my parents faced when they bought their home in 1948. The realtors and the home owners were reluctant to sell to us. I got that angry feeling all over again. In 1967 we were finally able to purchase our home in Daly City.

When I first went to work as an Iron Worker (1954), I didn't know anything about unions or apprenticeships, and I wanted to learn the trade. I didn't know that as a minority I had a very slim chance of getting into the apprenticeship training program, so I went to a good trade school and learned the trade that way. I also attended the Labor Management courses at the University of San Francisco. That angry feeling kept pushing me on. I later got involved in Union politics, and after thirty four years in the Iron Workers Union, I retired as the President of Shop Iron Workers Union Local 790 of the International Association of Bridge, Structural, and Ornamental Iron Workers AFL-CIO. Since my retirement in 1988 I've been a labor consultant for the AFL-CIO, and do a lot of motivational speaking at the high schools and middle schools, and have joined FAHNS (Filipino American National Historical Society).

Fred Basconcillo led the American Ironworkers Union for seventeen years. He was one of the few minorities in the national leadership of the AFL-CIO. He pushed aggressively to break the union-supported glass ceilings that excluded minorities from management-level positions. Leadership was part of his family tradition. His father, Artemio "Arte" Basconcillo, was a national president of the fraternal order of the Legionarios del Trabajo. His mother was Mary Velasco. His parents' home and restaurant together were a social-service center for Filipinos who were between jobs, looking for jobs, or facing deportation despite being U.S. nationals.

My generation, the baby boomers, owes a debt of gratitude to the silent generation. The latter served as a bridge to the pioneer generation before them. The silent generation was clearly aware of the sacrifices of those who went before them. They were dutiful sons and daughters who went on to multiply not just in terms of becoming parents but through their involvement in various aspects of American society, including education, employment, military service, organized labor, and home ownership. All this was accomplished within extended multiracial family settings, segregated neighborhoods, and in multicultural communities such as Seattle and San Francisco.

Beloved Children in the Land of Milk and Honey

The baby boomers, born between 1946 and 1964, were beloved and wanted children. Their parents had fought the good war. Their parents were sick of destruction and death, and they wanted life, love, and peace. So their parents went home, made babies, built the U.S. highway system, grew the economy, and fought the cold war, including Senator Joseph McCarthy and his House Un-American Activities Committee. But Filipino-American boomers were even luckier in my view. We were the beloved children of our fathers' old age and they raised us in the land of milk and honey. We were the children that many of our fathers thought they would never have. We were the children not only of our parents but of all the fledgling, extended families of Filipino Americans in the United States in the 1950s. We were the children of the bachelor Manongs who were our uncles, godfathers, and surrogate fathers. They babysat for us when our parents worked swing-shift hours. They listened to us, told us jokes, and gently reminded us to be good kids. Tata Pablo Placido, a nephew of my dad and viewed by my siblings and me as our second dad, took us to baseball games and wrestling matches. Lolo Frank Lazaro, my mom's uncle, bought us double scoops of homemade, hand-packed ice cream at the parlor near Onorato's Fish Market on Fillmore Street. They took us to Steinhart Aquarium, Golden Gate Park, and to planetarium programs at the California Academy of Sciences. They paid for our endless rides on the grand nineteenth-century carousel at the children's playground in Golden Gate Park. They drove us to the country—to Arroyo Grande, Pismo Beach, Delano, Stockton, Watsonville, and Porterville—so we could see where they spent their youth and meet our multiracial farm cousins. Tata Pablo and Lolo Faustino Lucas also took my family to Disneyland, Knott's Berry Farm, Marineland, and Universal Studios. They brought us to Stanford University, the University of California, Berkeley, the University of California, Los Angeles, and the state capitol in Sacramento.

They played with us on Marina Green overlooking the Golden Gate Bridge. They always remembered our birthdays, graduations, and Christmas with crisp ten- and twenty-dollar bills for our education fund. They taught me a song whose refrain I sang to myself and to my children many times, "Pretend you're happy, when you're blue. It isn't very hard to do. The world is mine. It can't be yours my friend. So why don't you pretend." Most important, with twinkles in their eyes, they told us we could be anyone and anything we wanted to be.

There were some couples like my parents who managed to marry before the war. My dad was forty-one when he went back to the Philippines to marry my mom at twenty-five, after several years of courtship. My Lola Basilisa, my maternal grandmother, thought my mom was too young to marry right after high school, and my mom thought my dad was too old for her. But, like a typical man of the "greatest generation," he convinced her to marry him when he said, "Ading[1] Aning, don't you know that love begins at forty?" My mother was pregnant with my sister, Roni, when dad returned to work in San Francisco, thinking that he would bring his family to the United States after my sister's birth. But the Japanese government bombed Pearl Harbor and invaded the Philippines. Like many newlyweds, my parents were separated during the war years, delaying family formation. After the war, they and many other couples of their generation caught up on lost time by producing the largest U.S. birth cohort in the twentieth century.

For many years, when Filipino-American boomers were growing up, many of our fathers worked more than one job. This was not unusual for men of color with historically lower wages than white men. For example, my dad held a full-time union job as an apartment building janitor during the day. After dinner, he'd work three to four hours at a downtown restaurant as a waiter or dishwasher. He also did handyman work on weekends. Many of our mothers were eager to work for three reasons. First, they were usually better educated than their older husbands. My mother graduated from high school, my father from elementary school. Of my aunts who were college-educated teachers and nurses, their spouses oftentimes were elementary- and high-school graduates. Better education correlates with higher labor-force participation rates. Second, our parents came from a Philippine culture that supported women working outside the home. After graduation from high school, my mom, a young, single woman, applied for and won a coveted position as a census worker. She went to the barrios for her field enumeration. She was accompanied by her mother, who served as her chaperone, cook, and laundress. In keeping with this tradition of wage-earning women in the Philippines, Filipina-American women and overseas Filipino domestic workers continue to have some of the highest labor-force participation rates of all women.

Third, and I think most important, is that my mother and aunts, like other racial- and ethnic-minority groups and upwardly mobile immigrants before them, wanted to help their husbands achieve and secure middle-class status for their families. They wanted to ensure that their children would partake fully of all the rights and responsibilities of a U.S. citizenship that they themselves did not have as children. My mom worked full time as a nonunion beautician, working ten-hour days from the time my baby brother was three years old until a year after he graduated from law school. Many of us baby boomers spent some time as latchkey kids cared for by our older siblings, who were surrogate parents. My brother, Bill, and I often feel that we were raised as much by Roni, our older sister, as by our parents. Indeed, we were raised by a village of parents, siblings, bachelor Manongs, Manangs, and married aunts and uncles.

We were also babysat by television shows, ranging from Dave Garroway and Florence Henderson on the *Today Show*, and *Captain Kangaroo* and *Rocky and Bullwinkle* before school, to *Queen for a Day*, Johnny Carson's *Who Do You Trust?*, *The Millionaire*, and the *Mouseketeers* after school. My friend Rita Cacas and her three siblings were raised in the post–World War II Filipino-American community of Oxon Hill, Maryland. They had other babysitters. Her dad retired from the navy and worked for decades as a Washington, D.C., taxi driver to support his growing family. On weekday mornings, he would drive his wife to work and drop Rita and her siblings off at their parish church, where the Cacas children attended two consecutive masses before their parochial school opened for class.

So that my parents could have a few hours alone on Saturday afternoons, my sister and I walked two blocks to Tata Bill and Nana Turina's home, which had a television. Roni and I were entertained by cowboys—Roy Rogers and Dale Evans, the Cisco Kid, the Lone Ranger, Johnny Mack Brown, Kit Carson, Sky King, and John Wayne. Weeknights when our mother hadn't yet come home from the beauty shop and my dad had to take Roni to Napa for doctor's appointments, Bill and I kept company with Walt Disney's *El Fuego Baca*, *Zorro*, and Cochise in *Broken Arrow*. In addition to the urban village of the Filipino-American community, the formative years of the Filipino-American baby boomers were influenced by other external institutions, namely the Catholic Church and its parochial schools.

Morning Star School, then Mercy High School

Parochial schools for their offspring were a logical choice for pioneer-generation parents. The Catholic Church was for them a principal form of social order dating to Spanish colonization. In the Philippines, children of the elite were sent to parochial schools from kindergarten to university. In the United States, in the segregated, lower-income neighborhoods of Filipino Americans, the church and its parish schools were familiar and protective institutions. Morning Star

School was founded in the 1930s by the Order of the Divine Word, a Jesuit offshoot. Divine Word priests were known as missionaries to Japan. Morning Star and its parish, St. Francis Xavier Church, served the growing Japanese-American community in San Francisco, which was located between the predominantly black Western Addition neighborhood and exclusively white Pacific Heights. The priests were of German ancestry and fluent in at least four languages—German, Latin, English, and Japanese. The nuns of Morning Star were from a Belgian order, the Daughters of Mary and Joseph. Most were of Irish ancestry, having escaped the poverty of Ireland. There were also a very few white American nuns and one Mexican-American nun from the southern California novitiate. When Japanese Americans were interned in federal camps during World War II, then pastor of Morning Star School, William Stoecke, opened the school up to the neighborhood children: Filipinos, Chinese, Mexicans, American Indians, blacks, and whites. At the same time, some of the Daughters of Mary and Joseph volunteered to go to the camps with their Morning Star students and other students from the Los Angeles area. After the war and following the return of Japanese Americans from the camps, Morning Star gradually returned to being a mostly Japanese-American school. The school's parent-teacher association was led by nisei, or second-generation Japanese Americans, some of whom were graduates of California's public colleges and universities, and, equally important, were members of the Japanese American Citizens League, a pioneer national Asian-American organization formed to advocate full constitutional and citizenship rights for Asian Americans.

While the landmark 1954 Supreme Court decision *Brown v. Board of Education* was being fought and won in black and white America, my siblings, cousins, neighbors, and I went to school in the 1950s and 1960s with a multicultural, multiracial, multilingual student body—and also an interracial one. The Amerasian children of Asian war brides and U.S. soldiers from World War II and the Korean War began to populate Morning Star. These Asian-American students were taught by nuns and priests, particularly, Rev. Joseph Guetzloe, who themselves were multilingual, multicultural, and ecumenical, and who taught us all to be Americans. When we were studying world history in the sixth grade, Sister Miriam Henrietta asked us to think about what the skin color of the historical Jesus might have been. We gave her all sorts of answers and explanations. Her answer surprised us. Sister Miriam Henrietta told us that since Jesus was a man of the Middle East, she imagined his complexion was more like that of Filipinos. On our report cards, citizenship stood out as a major evaluation category, along with math and science. The nuns taught us the Irish jig and American square dances. Sisters Margaret Mary and Celestine jumped rope with the girls and played baseball with the boys. Every Tuesday, a lady from Bank of America in a gray, fitted suit came and solemnly stamped our savings account books as we gave her our hard-earned dimes and quarters. Every morning, we lined up on the playground by grade and height to say our morning prayers. This was followed by the eighth-grade captain of the traffic boys raising the American flag up the flag pole as we recited the Pledge of Allegiance with right hands on our hearts.

Sisters Mary Colm and Brigid Mary were as excited as my fifth-grade class when Alan Shepard, Gus Grissom, and John Glenn went into space. They were ecstatic when John Fitzgerald Kennedy won the Democratic presidential nomination in 1960 and then went on to be president. Not only was he a descendant of Irish immigrants, but he was a Catholic as well. Given the discrimination against Catholics in the early decades of the United States and the severe discrimination against Irish immigrants and their descendants in the nineteenth and early twentieth centuries, this was a milestone.

From Morning Star, many graduates moved on to public or private school. I moved on to Mercy High School. Mercy High School is located in one of the higher-income neighborhoods of San Francisco, across the street from Stonestown Mall and just north of San Francisco State University. In the fall of 1962, Mercy High School had an enrollment of eight hundred girls. Most of them were white. Students of color could be counted on one hand. The junior-class president, however, was the light-skinned daughter of a prominent black physician. The other nonwhite in the junior class was a Filipino-American girl whose father was in the military. There was one Filipino-American daughter of a diplomat in the sophomore class. In my freshman class, there were Pat Ige, a Japanese American from Hawaii, and I. At this point, the handful of Hispanic students, were known as "Castilian" or white.

For baby boomer Filipino Americans in elite parochial and public schools of the time (my siblings graduated from nationally known Lowell High School), our connection to primarily white (and at Lowell, Chinese and Jewish) classmates was through American culture. We connected through the San Francisco Giants and the San Francisco 49ers, through Motown music, the Apollo missions, the British invasion lead by the Beatles, and through a young, good-looking American couple, Jack and Jackie Kennedy. In addition, Catholic schools connected us to our faith through another John: Pope John XXIII, who gave us Vatican II and who asked Catholics to refocus on the essence of Christianity, including the role of laity in Catholicism. As parochial-school students, we were also impressed by the growing civil rights movement led by ministers who practiced nonviolence and who demanded social justice in the tradition of Jesus Christ. It was my teachers at Mercy High School—nuns, priests, and laity—who told me and my classmates of an antebellum history of female black slaves raped by white owners, of the Dred Scott decision that declared that blacks, free or slave, could not become U.S. citizens (*Dred Scott v. Sanford*, 1857), and of the impact of *Plessy v. Ferguson* (see chap. 2). My junior-year U.S.-history teacher, Mrs. Sindell, the first Jewish teacher at Mercy High School, wife of a University of California Boalt Law School professor, and an ACLU officer, made us think about the constitutionality of the Japanese-American internment and the merits and drawbacks of legalized prostitution. On retreats, we were shown films such as *Harvest of Shame*, and we read Michael Harrington's *The Other America*. We were sent to participate with fellow students from around the Bay Area in seminars and workshops on civil rights, race relations, poverty in affluence, and the rights of farm workers. As children born after the atomic bomb, we debated the question of whether nuclear weapons were a deterrent of or a catalyst for war.

On the other hand, one of our classmates left school as a pregnant sophomore. She joined us at our graduation in June 1966 with her young son to warm greetings from students, faculty, and staff. The only other fifteen-year-old mother that I knew when I was fifteen was the daughter of one of my mom's relatives. It was a striking moment in my life. Their family had been over to our home for dinner, and Aurora (pseudonym) and I had been looking at teen magazines and Katy Keene and Archie comic books. A few months later, my parents and I visited her family with baby presents. There was Aurora, a couple of months older than me, giving her new baby boy his milk bottle. Suddenly, I was no longer worried but looked forward to taking the PSAT and preparing for college.

ATTAINING HIGHER EDUCATION

While many of the silent-generation Filipino Americans entered the workforce upon high-school graduation, the baby boomers, particularly in California, with its free and high-quality public education, set their sights on college. This was poor timing because boomers of all backgrounds were contemplating college just as access to higher education in California was curtailed. As a means of controlling the increasing enrollment of GI Bill veterans and their children, as well as that of migrants from other states, the California State Legislature passed "The Master Plan for Higher Education in California: 1960–1975" (Barlow and Shapiro 1971, 27–32). The plan was based on three tiers that controlled who would have access to higher education. Half of the students who were projected to go to college between 1960 and 1975 would be diverted to junior colleges, which were paid for by local, not state, revenues.

> Diverting them was to be accomplished by jacking up the entrance requirements of the four year colleges so that the state colleges, previously open to between 50 and 70 percent of California's high school graduates, would now admit only the top 33 percent of the graduating seniors, while U.C., previously ready to accommodate 15 percent, was now closed to all but the top 12 per cent. All applicants to the four year colleges would be required to take the Scholastic Aptitude

Tests, which would determine their percentile rating according to a uniform national standard against which all students would be evaluated competitively. (Barlow and Shapiro 1971, 28–29)

In 1960, public higher education in California began a tradition of segmented access: two-year junior or community colleges that were open to any resident high-school graduate; four-year state colleges awarding primarily bachelor degrees and teaching credentials and offering a few masters programs; and the University of California campuses, which offered doctoral and professional programs and had renowned research centers, with the University of California, Berkeley, as the flagship. While there were student fees, there was no tuition for state residents. On the other hand, admissions requirements became more stringent and began to correlate with the decrease in the enrollment of all lower-income students, and particularly that of black and other racial-minority students.

Despite these obstacles, educational opportunity was still the way to upward mobility. A critical mass of second-generation Filipino Americans took advantage of the community colleges that provided business and technical curricula for immediate employment as well as courses parallel to the University of California, Berkeley, freshman and sophomore requirements. The latter arrangement allowed students to transfer to the state colleges or universities while commuting from home. Such inclusive public higher education policies in various states, including California, New York, and Michigan, facilitated the access of children of the working class to credentialed professions and first-class citizenship. What our Filipino-American parents and other racial-minority or working-class white parents could only dream of, our generation was going to achieve despite barriers and obstacles: an American college education. This is what my dad called "writing your own meal ticket" and being free to do whatever you wanted. In particular, my parents were ahead of their time in advocating that my sister and I not only attend college but also consider graduate school and, in any event, be able to support ourselves and our children. They did not want us to be dependent upon a male breadwinner because their experience had taught them that illness, death, desertion, job loss, and other calamities could happen at any time. Besides, our Filipina mothers and aunts felt that economic power was important if we were to be an equal partner in our marriages. Our parents pointed out to Roni and me various women, including the nuns who taught us, who had master's and professional degrees.

On Strike! Shut It Down!

Against the background of these changes in the availability of public higher education, the student strike at San Francisco State can be viewed as another historic event in the tension between Manifest Destiny and common destiny.

Public education is the road to upward economic mobility and to full civic participation. Denial of public education would not do for the post–World War II generations. Second-class citizenship would not do for the children of veterans. The desire of working-class whites and racial minorities for a college education and the expectation that they should be trained for postindustrial jobs were the American equivalent of revolutions that were occurring simultaneously around the world against colonialism, and were a counterpart to rising expectations of self-determination in former European colonies in the Third World.

Second-generation Filipino Americans watched the news as blacks in the South courageously challenged racial segregation in public institutions under the leadership coalition of the National Association for the Advancement of Colored People (NAACP), the Southern Christian Leadership Conference, the Student Nonviolent Coordinating Committee, and others; and they watched James Meredith attempt, as an individual, albeit with federal marshals and armed forces, to integrate the University of Mississippi. We were struck by the youthfulness of the civil rights movement. The Reverend Martin Luther King Jr. was in his thirties. Undergraduate and graduate students from historically black colleges, including U.S. Congressman John Lewis and the Reverend Jesse Jackson, were on the front lines. This revolution of rising expectations reverberated around the world as formerly colonized new nations in Africa and Asia freed themselves from Western colonialism, establishing democracies of self-rule and self-determination. Young people across the nation, including Filipino Americans, saw the power of youth nationally and globally. The ability to harness and organize this power was their challenge. In the late 1960s, children of the pioneer generation in California took on this challenge successfully through two organizations, the Philippine American Collegiate Endeavor (PACE) at San Francisco State and the Filipino American Young Turks of Seattle (FAYTS).

The Philippine American Collegiate Endeavor

PACE was an on-campus student organization at San Francisco State founded by Patrick Salaver, Ron Quidachay, Robert Ilumin, and Alex Soria. Its initial goals were tutoring young Filipino high school students from lower-income San Francisco neighborhoods and recruiting college applicants from the Filipino-American community (Barlow and Shapiro 1971, 157). Filipino-American students at four-year colleges at that point were few in number. We stood out because of our rarity. I was pleasantly surprised and excited to see Filipino faces on campus. But not just any Filipino faces. They were the faces of students with childhoods like mine. We were teenagers and twenty-year-olds, either born in the Philippines and brought to the United States as babies and toddlers or born in the United States. We had grown up in Salinas, Stockton, San Francisco, Daly City, or Vallejo. Most of our fathers were much older than our mothers. They were veterans and union members, and many were cooks, dishwashers, janitors, or all three.

PACE was one of the student organizations in the Third World Liberation Front (TWLF) that joined with the Black Students' Union (BSU), the initial leader of the 1968–1969 student strike at San Francisco State. This strike was the last in a series of initiatives over several years designed to address the declining enrollment of blacks, other minorities, and working-class students in general who were seeking higher education (Orrick 1969). In addition to seeking greater numbers of nonwhite students (whose proportion of the student population was minimal), the student strike demanded a School of Ethnic Studies, including a Black Studies Department, and greater admissions of students from nontraditional populations—including nonwhite students, rural students, and lower-income students (Boyle 1970; Orrick 1969; Barlow and Shapiro 1971, 156, app. 1). A School of Ethnic Studies was viewed as necessary if, once admitted, minority students were to stay in college and graduate. After all, many would be the first in their families and communities to go to college. The strikers demanded a curriculum that reflected the history and contributions of people of color to the United States. They also demanded slots for faculty and administrators who acknowledged and understood the status of minority populations, particularly those who came from these populations. It was not an unreasonable conclusion that minority faculty and administrators could be more effective role models and mentors to the nontraditional, underprivileged student populations than would be traditionally privileged white males. In the 1960s and 1970s, there were very few white female and minority male professors, let alone minority female ones. In addition, given the heterogeneity of California's demography and California's global stature, students, faculty, and community leaders agreed that all students should know the history, heritage, and contributions of diverse California settlers before they went into the work force to serve and interact with various communities.

Later on, TWLF joined with other white-led student groups to oppose the war in Vietnam, Laos, and Cambodia. PACE leaders were pivotal in TWLF, the coalition that negotiated with the college and state administrators. It was the leaders of PACE, several of whom were mestizos, who kept the often contentious student organizations from fragmenting into separate interests. There were several reasons for PACE's role as unifier. One was that the leaders of PACE could identify across groups, having grown up with blacks in Fillmore, Latinos in the Mission, American Indians in the San Joaquin Valley, the Japanese in "J-Town," and the whites in "the avenues." Several PACE members were Filipino-black, Filipino-American Indian, and Filipino-white. Many of us had Chinese or Spanish grandparents, and some of us were raised in Latino traditions and the Spanish language. Another reason was that our dads' military experience and union-organizing work had demanded equality and representation from diverse groups using due process and by working toward a common goal. Certainly we knew well the pivotal role Filipino-American farm workers had played in achieving such goals. In 1965 union leaders, notably Philip Vera Cruz and Larry Itliong, working with the Agricultural Workers Organizing Committee of the AFL-CIO, supported Filipino farm workers in their sit-down strike in the Coachella vineyards. The strike launched what was to become the United Farm Workers Union (UFW) as it moved north to Delano. While Mexican-American Cesar Chavez was the most visible leader of the UFW, it was the Filipino-American leaders, much as during the time of Carlos Bulosan, who consistently stressed organizational unity and worker equity (Scharlin and Villaneuva 1992). Finally, our Catholic upbringing during the time of Vatican II encouraged us to question tradition and to acknowledge contemporary concerns for the need of inclusiveness, tolerance, and social justice. We also borrowed liberally from liberation theology.

Equally important were our Filipino values and our emphasis on smooth personal relations and saving face. For example, the male PACE members would occasionally accentuate our discussions with four-letter words, not surprising given the influence of the Free Speech Movement at neighboring University of California, Berkeley. Invariably, however, they would quickly apologize to their "Pinay sisters" and other women for disrespectful language and treatment. In addition, the "Bayannihan" spirit prevailed as we held poster parties; wrote, typed, printed, and distributed leaflets about the strike; cracked self-effacing jokes; played music; and hosted intercultural programs. No less important perhaps was the fact that our parents' generation supported our student activism. By the late 1960s, the mainly working-class pioneer generation had been joined by new immigrants from professional and business backgrounds. These adults formed a formidable parental collective conscience. Similarly, the Japanese-American and black students were supported by their parents and communities who saw similarities between the forced incarceration of mainland Japanese Americans during World War II, depriving them of their constitutional rights and the forced segregation of blacks in the United States (Orrick 1969, 119–21). The *Philippine News* featured PACE's tutoring programs for newly arrived Filipino immigrant youth and highlighted PACE student leadership in establishing in 1969 the first Pilipino American Studies undergraduate program in the United States. The Philippine Consulate in San Francisco, especially then Consul General Samson Sabalones, himself a former student leader, was always supportive in providing meeting space and encouraging dialogue between student leaders and established community leaders, between the American-born and the Philippine-born.

Changes Ensue at Elite Institutions of Higher Education

The student strike at San Francisco State did not go unnoticed. Other campuses across the United States also went on strike. Ethnic Studies programs, particularly Black Studies programs, were begun. Students of color were recruited for higher education. PACE members worked with students and faculty at City College of San Francisco, other Bay Area community colleges, University of California, Berkeley, and University of California, Los Angeles, to increase admissions of minority students and to include courses in Ethic Studies programs—that reflected the role and experiences of these populations in American history and society—among the list of selections necessary to fulfill general graduation requirements.

Suddenly in the 1970s, recruiters from elite institutions of higher education were meeting with the student leaders of color at undergraduate public institutions like San Francisco State—that is, with nontraditional recruitment sources. Minority recruiters came from University of California, Berkeley, University of California, Los Angeles, Stanford University, the University of Chicago, Cornell University, Columbia University, and other institutions. We were told to consider graduate school as an option for making institutional changes from within the system. These outreach actions by elite institutions were the beginning of the entry of working-class, second-generation Filipino Americans and other racial minorities into elite U.S. graduate schools and professional schools of law and medicine.

AMERICAN SOCIAL ORDER AND ECONOMIC WELL-BEING

The second generation of Filipino Americans were also beneficiaries of their parental generation's sacrifices for freedom and equal opportunity. In their own right, their parents shaped the American social order away from a traditional hierarchy of a privileged, white, Anglo-Saxon Protestant establishment at the top toward a more level playing field. While the San Francisco second generation was beginning to coalesce, the Seattle second generation was firmly a player in moving the wider Seattle community toward a common destiny.

The Filipino American Young Turks of Seattle

An advantage of the Seattle second generation of Filipino Americans was that they started earlier and had a critical mass. Unlike the primarily post–World War II San Francisco Filipino-American community, there was an identifiable community of Filipino-American families in Seattle by the 1930s. While

Filipino men married both Filipino and non-Filipino women, a sizable portion
of white mothers chose to raise their children in the Filipino-American community. Many of these families lived in racially segregated neighborhoods
with other minority groups, especially Japanese Americans. These second-
generation Filipino-American children were neighbors, playmates, and classmates of second-generation Japanese Americans. Called the nisei generation
(Lyman 1973), these U.S.-born children of *issei*—Japanese pioneer
generation—parents, shared with Filipino Americans similar experiences in
growing up. They were a generation of children whose parents were migrants,
were neither black nor white, and were viewed as foreign, not American. A
similar phenomenon occurred in Hawaii, where second-generation Japanese
and Filipino Americans played and grew up together before World War II as
their parents worked on the plantations. These two groups formed a
post–World War II leadership of Asian Americans who successfully gained
access to the mainstream by working in coalitions with other Americans.

Peter Jamero described the Seattle second-generation Filipino-American
leaders via the Filipino American Young Turks of Seattle (FAYTS).

> The seeds of the FAYTS movement were sown in the civil rights decade of the
> 1960s. Activists who would later become key FAYTS players participated as in-
> dividuals in marches and demonstrations supporting causes in what then was
> largely focused on other ethnic group concerns. Their participation gave them
> valuable lessons in dealing with mainstream America in terms of tactics and
> strategy. More important, Filipino American participation in the civil rights
> movement provided visibility and lasting credibility in working with Seattle's
> major ethnic minorities—black, Hispanic, Asian, and Native American. By the
> end of the 1960s, a number of Filipino Americans had taken on visible profes-
> sional and community responsibilities. Bob Santos was appointed to the Seattle
> Human Rights Commission, Roy Flores became the first director of the Ethnic
> Cultural Center at the University of Washington, and Anthony Ogilvie was
> named assistant director of Office of Minority Affairs at Seattle University.
> (Jamero 1997, 301–2)

This coalition work across various populations was transferred to Filipino-
American social and civic participation by 1970, when Tony Barruso cam-
paigned for Washington State representative. As Jamero noted,

> The Barruso campaign was the first sociopolitical activity in which FAYTS col-
> lective knowledge, professional skills, and community networks were focused
> on a Filipino American issue. By 1970, these Young Turks had developed into a
> close-knit group who were looking for means to move Filipino Americans onto
> center stage. Prior to 1970, they played largely supporting roles to other ethnic
> groups. Now they wanted to open doors for Filipinos to participate in the so-
> ciopolitical mainstream. This common concern for Filipino access to, and em-

powerment in, institutions in the wider community was the single most important defining factor that drew these young Filipinos Americans together. It was their major common and sustaining bond. However, the group had other factors in common:

Most had roots in the Central Area, the inner-city district where Seattle's ethnic minorities were concentrated and where the heart of the initial Filipino community was first situated.

They attended common schools: Maryknoll and St. Theresa Catholic grade schools, Immaculate and O'Dea Catholic high schools, and Franklin and Garfield high schools.

Virtually all were well educated and well read. Most had earned at a least a bachelor's degree, and some were in the midst of master's or doctorate programs.

Most were associated as youths with Filipino Youth Activities of Seattle, Inc. (FYA), where they first learned to bond and share an uncommon trust with one another.

They had strong credibility with other ethnic communities.

There existed an effective skill level of relating with the dominant white community nurtured through their experience in the world of work and the broader community.

The group was relatively young; most were in their early 30s.

All but one were American born, and only one had ever visited the Philippines. They identified themselves as Filipino Americans; their concerns were American issues. (Jamero 1997, 302–3)

In many ways, the members of FAYTS were similar to members of the PACE generation.

PARENTS TO THE THIRD GENERATION, GRANDPARENTS TO THE FOURTH

The second generation accomplished their parents' dreams. That is, by and large they achieved full entry into American society. This is not to deny that there are disadvantaged segments of this population. But they were fortunate to grow up at a time of economic growth in the United States and during the civil rights movements spanning the era of the New Deal in the 1930s through the Great Society of the 1960s and 1970s. In my view, these societal events defined their ability to succeed as much as did their parents' and communities' support. Both segregation and equal opportunity advanced this generation's ability to be involved with a more multicultural society and to interact with other classes.

Along with other baby boomers, second-generation Filipino Americans were also defined by the Vietnam War as they made the transition from innocent youth to sobering adulthood. Overall, the second generation became part of the American mainstream. They continued their parents' move outside segregated neighborhoods to "the avenues" and then to the suburbs; rural second-generation children moved to cities for schools just as the Filipino-American population permanently shifted from rural to urban residence; and our Hawaii cousins were sent to the mainland for school and to join the mainstream.

The second generation had opportunities for education beyond high school and for a larger array of occupational and career choices than their parents. Embedded in the military, in large corporations, and in the medical industry and union-protected occupations, the second generation assumed salaried positions with benefits such as pensions and health insurance. They continued to maintain high rates of labor-force participation, increasing rates of home ownership, and strong commitments to marriage and family. While a good number of their spouses and children continued to be Filipino, they also contributed to growing numbers and proportions of non-Filipino spouses and children. Many still chose to have Catholic weddings, to have their children baptized, and to send their children to parochial schools. They continued to maintain extended family ties. Many of their pioneer-generation parents served as occasional or primary babysitters and presided over social gatherings and family dinners. Three generations of Filipino Americans and their extended families then gathered around the dinner tables of these pioneer-generation grandparents. Such day-to-day activities ensured the continuation of generations of Filipino Americans in the United States and, equally as important, ensured a Filipino-American heritage for the third and fourth generations.

THE SECOND GENERATION'S IMPACT ON AMERICA

The second generation of Filipino Americans was composed of the silent generation and baby boomer cohorts. They spanned a birth period lasting from the Depression through the post–World War II affluence. They grew up loved by their extended families as they navigated growing up as racial minorities in the United States in the 1940s, 1950s, and 1960s. Expanding on the foundation that their parents had given them of secure full rights and responsibilities as Americans, they entered the American mainstream first through the New Deal and then via the various equal-opportunity policies and programs of the Great Society. This period of American history focused on the common destiny of all residents of the United States. Since then, the statutes and programs of equality from this era have been constantly challenged, first through litigation, starting with *Bakke v. The University of California* in 1976, and then through revised interpretations of civil rights policies. The second generation of Filipino Americans were beneficiaries of one of the greatest periods of peace and prosperity in U.S. history. They were part of the American generation who said, "Make love, not war." Like their parents returning from World War II, this generation, after the war in Southeast Asia, went off with their partners to have the children who would become the next generation of Filipino Americans. However, the formation of the Filipino-American population was not linear. As the baby boomer segment of the second generation came of age, a new group of Filipinos migrated to the United States, forcing Filipino Americans to again reexamine the tensions of Manifest Destiny and common destiny.

NOTES

1. *Ading* means "younger sibling" in Ilocano.

Chapter Four

Flying across Skies:
The Post-1965 Immigrant Generation

In 1964 my mother, no longer a Philippine citizen but a brand-new American citizen, took her first trip back to the Philippines. She brought my siblings and me with her. Our father threw a *despedida* (going away) party and, with a host of aunts, uncles, and cousins, saw us board a Pan American Airlines clipper at San Francisco International Airport. We traveled via Hawaii, where we were introduced to Pearl City cousins, and refueled in Guam. Of the four of us, I think, Roni was the best adjusted to the Philippines. She had fond memories of being there as a child, and many friends and loving aunts and uncles whom she was looking forward to being reunited and reconnected with. Bill and I were in culture shock, never having seen so many Filipinos in our lives. Our mom was overcome equally, with great joy, to see relatives and friends, but also with profound sadness to witness the socioeconomic disparity between life in the Philippines and life in the United States. Yet at that point the Philippines had one of the healthier Asian economies, second only to Japan, with a highly educated English-speaking work force familiar with American culture and displaying a keen interest in U.S. and world news. Several of our first and second cousins on my mom's side were doing well and were bound for, or were already in, college in Manila. This was the pre-Marcos period.

Immigration to the United States was a constant topic of discussion among adults of labor-force age in the Philippines, including our social-worker cousin Ciony, her college-educated friends working in professional positions, and our Uncle Lynn, who was soon to be eligible to retire from the Philippine Air Force. They were aware of proposed amendments to the 1952 McCarran-Walter Act, which had upheld the 1924 National Origins Act, including an immigration quota system that favored Northern and Western Europeans (Dimas, Chou, and Fong 1980, 9). On the other hand, the McCarran-Walter Act articulated the three principles of U.S. immigration policy that are still in effect: (1) the reunification of families, (2) the protection of the domestic labor force, and (3) the immigration of persons with needed skills (1980, 11). The amendments passed by Congress in 1965 had abolished the national origins system as well as the Asiatic barred zone (1980, 11). With these amendments, "Congress created a seven category preference system giving immigration priority to relatives of United States residents and immigrants with needed talents or skills" (1980, 11). Taken together with subsequent changes in immigration and refugee policies in the latter half of the twentieth century, the demographic impact on both the general U.S. population and specific subpopulations, such as Filipino Americans, has been tremendous and long term.

In June 1966, Catalino Paguirigan Lucas, my Uncle Lynn, arrived in San Francisco, sponsored by my parents under the fifth preference in the allotment of immigrant visas for family-sponsored immigrants (brothers and sisters of U.S. citizens). He lived with us for several months, found a job stocking merchandise at the Emporium on Market Street, became acclimated to San Francisco weather, and adjusted with both grace and difficulty to a new stage of life as an older immigrant with a lower status than he had held in the Philippines. By 1970 Uncle Lynn had earned and saved enough to bring his wife and four children to the United States. This process of chain migration was repeated in other Filipino-American communities as U.S. citizens and permanent residents petitioned for their spouses, children, siblings, and parents.

LINKING PRE-1965 SETTLERS TO NEW IMMIGRANTS

At the time, I did not think about the significance of the "coming to America" of the Lucas family. As an adult, however, I am beginning to understand and appreciate this second migration of Filipinos to America. On a personal level, I am again impressed by the vast knowledge, ability, skills, patience, and perseverance of my parents and their peers who were able to take advantage of public policies and work within the administrative and bureaucratic process. On a collective level, the post-1965 generation ensured the continuation of Filipino Americans demographically. This is a crucial point in my view. That is, without the post-1965 immigrants, the Filipino-American community could have disappeared. While the silent generation and baby boomer cohorts were forming families and raising the third generation, they were still a small number and a minuscule fraction of the U.S. population. Coupled with a greater tendency to marry non-Filipinos, when compared with other racial minorities, and greater access to the mainstream, the Filipino-American population could have declined and even decreased by the third and fourth generation, along the lines of the sansei and the yonsei, the third and fourth generations, respectively, of Japanese Americans described by Harry Kitano (1969).

The effect of the post-1965 generation, in cooperation with the first pioneer generation, who supported and sponsored many of them, was increased numbers and a greater proportion of Filipino Americans, relative to U.S. population, through births and migration. In the 1970 U.S. Census, there were 343,000 Filipinos. They were the smallest of the three major Asian-American populations, with the Japanese as the largest followed by the Chinese. After the post-1965 revisions in immigration laws and refugee policies emanating from the Vietnam War, the Asian-American population became larger and more diverse. By the 1990 U.S. Census and continuing into the 2000 U.S. Census, Filipinos, with a population of 2 million, were the second-largest Asian-American population after the Chinese. In contrast, with minimal migration from Japan, the Japanese-American population was not even in the top five groups (Asian Indian, Vietnamese, and Korean were the other larger groups). By the 2000 U.S. Census, the Japanese-American population was decreasing proportionally and numerically due to minimal, almost nil, immigration, decreasing birth rates, and the persistence of interethnic (with other Asians) and interracial unions.

THE ROLE OF CHAIN MIGRATION FOR MULTIPLE GENERATIONS OF FILIPINO AMERICANS

The immigration policies of the United States have evolved over time to meet the needs of this nation from its beginning as a demographically white Anglo-Saxon Protestant population working within an agrarian and industrial capitalistic economy with self-rule via a representative government. The labor required to meet these needs in a vast, diverse, and sparsely populated land mass included the forced migration of slaves from Africa, beginning in the seventeenth century, the migration of indentured servants from Europe in the eighteenth century, and the migration of low-wage earners from non-Anglo-Saxon European countries in the nineteenth century. With the construction of the transcontinental railroad and development of the West and Southwest in the mid-nineteenth century, migration commenced across the Pacific and the Rio Grande. In the postindustrial, global economy of the twentieth and twenty-first centuries, a competitive United States draws on three labor pools: native-born workers, immigrants living in the United States, and citizens or permanent residents of other nations working as outsourced labor. Given the global economy, it is not always easy to distinguish U.S. work from other work because of transnational connections and the interdependence of equipment, labor, capital, and the production process across nation-states. Another

complexity is that these three labor pools may or may not be stratified occu-
pationally by ancestry, race, or citizenship.

In comparing the status of nineteenth-century European immigrants with
that of nineteenth- and twentieth-century Southern blacks migrating to the
North and Puerto Ricans migrating to the mainland, social scientists have
studied the employment and economic context in which the descendants of
these two populations grew. Portes has summarized these underlying effects:

> The nation takes care of its immediate labor needs, as defined by powerful
> global interests, and lets the future take care of itself. A fortunate combination
> of circumstances, including an expanding economy, a scarcity of labor due to a
> new global conflict, and other factors, allowed the European second generation
> to move steadily up the American economic and social ladders. Their generally
> successful experience was subsequently captured in academic theories, includ-
> ing the concept of a linear process of assimilation. Children of southern black
> and Puerto Rican migrants arriving later in the century were less fortunate. A
> different set of circumstances, including widespread discrimination and a
> changing economy blocked the mobility of these migrants' children and con-
> fined many to the same inferior job held by their parents. The perpetuation of
> these negative conditions eventually led to an interrelated set of urban patholo-
> gies. These experiences gave rise to different academic theories, including the
> concept of a culture of poverty and the urban underclass (Moynihan 1969; Wil-
> son 1987; Gans 1990; Jencks 1992). (Portes 1996, 5)

The status of the Filipino-American generations that followed the pioneer
generation provides yet another picture of life chances for nonwhite Anglo-
Saxon Protestant migrants to the United States. In the twenty-first century, as
younger immigration researchers study the new immigrant generations from
Africa, eastern Europe, Latin America, the Middle East, South Asia, and
Southeast Asia, they are adding to the observations and findings of Moynihan, Portes, and other social scientists (Foner, Rumbaut, and Gold 2000).

Despite the varying economic conditions that greet each wave of new
migrants, the post-1965 immigrants benefited from the fact that they were
part of, not the start of, a chain migration. A unique advantage of the post-
1965 immigrants is that they were not pioneers. They were not the first of
their group going to a new and unknown land. Rather, "the early roots of
the immigration stream—Filipino plantation workers imported to Hawaii
and California—provided a strong U.S. network that was able to take quick
advantage of the 1965 changes in the U.S. immigration law" (Fawcett and
Cariño 1987, 19). What is not commonly recognized is that the Manongs
and Manangs were not only instrumental in producing the second and subsequent generations of Filipino Americans but also facilitated the entry of
post-1965 immigrants to the United States.

Although small in number, these early streams of immigrants were significant in that they facilitated the entry of future immigrants through the family reunification provisions of the immigration laws . . . The importance of chain migration has grown for all countries in the region, and the vast majority of Southeast Asian immigrants now enter the United States under the family preference categories. (Cariño 1987, 310)

While some post-1965 immigrants, such as my cousin Ciony, were able to sponsor themselves as professionals with needed skills, many more were like my Uncle Lynn and were sponsored by a relative. For the pioneer generation who had a custom of sending remittances to help their families in the Philippines, sponsorship was an investment in the ability of their kin to earn a living in the United States. By coming to America, these immigrants could in turn become self-sufficient and then help to support other kin.

There were several preferences for persons who immigrated to the United States as the relative of a U.S. citizen or lawful resident alien, but only one preference for professionals, scientists, and artists of exceptional ability (Dimas, Chou, and Fong 1980, 11). Furthermore, those who were not directly sponsored by relatives nevertheless had access to the pioneer generation's knowledge and experiences in navigating a new land. Financial and other types of assistance were (and continue to be) commonly provided to the newcomers, whose income was initially in pesos, by the old-timers and their children, whose incomes were in dollars. That is, the post-1965 immigrants had access to the capital and networks of the earlier generations. Yet the post-1965 immigrants distinguished themselves from the pioneer generation because of socioeconomic and regional differences in the Philippines. The pioneer generation was generally less educated, hailed from the rural, working-class background of the Ilocos provinces and the Visayas, and spoke Ilocano and Visayan. The post-1965 immigrants were primarily better-educated urbanites speaking Pilipino or Tagalog. They viewed themselves as expatriates and Filipinos in America. By contrast, the pioneer generation and their descendants saw themselves as Americans with Filipino ancestry. The post-1965 generation was and may still be in limbo—not yet a part of the United States, nor a staying power in the Philippines.

THE CHOSEN PEOPLE OF THE PHILIPPINES

One of the frustrations often voiced by Philippine nationals in America and other countries is the lack of Filipino power in the Philippines, forcing them to go elsewhere for their children's future. (This is often true of other nationals migrating to the United States.) A popular rationale for this lack of power is that the Philippines has been an independent republic only since 1946. This may reasonably be viewed as an insufficient time period in which to overcome almost four centuries of colonization by Spain and the United States. An additional but less articulated reason is the long-term economic control in the Philippines by Chinese and Spanish minorities.

The Chinese in the Philippines

Yale law professor Amy Chua, writing on ethnic conflicts and democracy in global markets, notes that the Chinese hold economic power in much of Asia, including the Philippines.

> My family is part of the Philippines' tiny but entrepreneurial, economically powerful Chinese minority. Just 1 percent of the population, Chinese Filipinos control as much as 60 percent of the private economy, including the country's four major airlines and almost all of the country's banks, hotels, shopping malls, and major conglomerates. My own family in Manila runs a plastics conglomerate. Unlike taipans Lucio Tan, Henry Sy, or John Gokongwei, my relatives are only "third tier" Chinese tycoons. Still, they own swaths of prime real estate and several vacation homes . . .
>
> . . . In the Philippines, millions of Filipinos work for Chinese; almost no Chinese work for Filipinos. The Chinese dominate industry and commerce at every level of society. Global markets intensify this dominance. When foreign investors do business in the Philippines, they deal almost exclusively with Chinese. Apart from a handful of corrupt politicians and a few aristocratic Spanish mestizo families, all of the Philippines' billionaires are of Chinese descent. By contrast, all menial jobs in the Philippines are done by Filipinos. All peasants are Filipinos. All domestic servants and squatters are Filipinos. (Chua 2003, 3–4)

The Chinese share the title of "the chosen people of the Philippines" along with the Spaniards. The Chinese are stereotyped for their brain power and entrepreneurship. For example, some observers attribute former President Ferdinand Marcos's brilliance to his alleged father, a powerful Chinese Filipino. Former President Corazon Aquino's family, the Cojuangcos, originated in the Fujian province of China.

Spaniards in the Philippines

In contrast to the Chinese, whose superiority over Filipinos derives from entrepreneurial economic power, the Spaniards ruled the Philippines through the Catholic Church and by extracting natural resources for export via the Manila Galleon trade to Mexico and Spain.

Instead of evidence of commercial development, Spain's most lasting tangible imprint on Filipinos has been the Spanish Catholic world view and language. This thin overlay of European culture resulted in the hybridization of the indigenous cultural, religious, and linguistic practices, reproachably Western to neighboring Asians and confusing to Filipinos . . .

. . . The only commercial enterprise organized with some success was the previously mentioned galleon trade. For Spaniards in Manila, the galleon trade was singularly suitable: It required only graft (plentiful), capital (frequently borrowed or extorted from the local Chinese), and luck of good weather (courtesy of divine intervention). Of ingenuity and hard work it had no need. The Spaniards, after all, did not come to the island to become merchants or farmers; they were hidalgos. (Rimonte 1997, 51–52)[1]

DISPARITY WITHIN THE FILIPINO POPULATION

With the transfer of colonial control from Spain to the United States, Filipinos continued to be a numerical majority but a political and economic minority. In their own land, they were excluded from elite institutions and social clubs and from prime commercial and residential areas. Filipinos were servants to Spaniards, Chinese, and Americans. This disparity was played out within the Filipino population, where Filipino households from the upper class to the working class had servants. On our 1964 trip to the Philippines, my siblings and I remarked on how even the servants employed servants. Thus, while Filipinos were the racial majority in their country and indeed were well-represented in civic and electoral participation, higher education, and middle-class culture, they were a minority in the highest levels of institutional and legitimate economic and political power. Such a situation was ripe for emigration, fueling the diaspora of Filipinos around the world.

Filipinos as Voluntary and Involuntary Immigrants

The specific immigration of Filipinos to the United States must be viewed within the larger diaspora of Filipinos. U.S. history is traditionally taught as that of a nation of immigrants, with various populations coming to America voluntarily despite indigenous American Indians, earlier settlement by Spanish America, and the African slave trade. In recent decades, historians and immigration scholars have conducted their research in terms of a diaspora framework. Rather than using the receiving country as the unit of analysis, the sending country is the analytical base. Prominent examples of diaspora are the Jews, whose numbers are dispersed around the world, the overseas Chinese, particularly in Asia, and the overseas Asian Indians in Africa and Europe. More recently, the International Nikkei Research Project has documented and examined globalization, the people of Japanese descent in the Americas, and the movement of immigrants from Latin America to Japan (Hirabayashi, Kikumura-Yano, and Hirabayashi 2002). The study of migration and mobility of peoples around the world has posited a multidimensional chain of networks based on the assumption that as individuals, group members are traceable to an initial culture, ancestry, and land of origin.

The Filipino Diaspora

The diaspora of Filipinos since the pioneer generation can be viewed as both voluntary and involuntary. Certainly some of the *pensionados* and young men of the Roaring Twenties came to the United States willingly in the search for education and adventure. As noted in chapter 2, however, most of this generation came to escape a lifetime of poverty. While this involuntary migration of Filipinos was not the forced migration of Africans to the Americas, Filipinos did experience pressures to leave the Philippines.

> Beyond international ties and changes in U.S. immigration policy, there are internal push factors that have reinforced the contemporary patterns of international migration from the Philippines. These factors include population growth trends, internal migration and urbanization and, more recently, the worsening social and economic problems of the country. (Cariño 1987, 313)

A major political factor in the migration of Filipinos was President Ferdinand Marcos's declaration of martial law in 1972. Political dissidents and intellectuals left the Philippines for the Americas, Asia, and Europe in self-exile to protest his regime and for the immediate safety and well-being of their families.

Another incentive, this one economic, was one President Marcos himself promoted: Filipinos were encouraged to go abroad as overseas workers, given the inability of the Filipino economy to provide jobs for its highly educated work force (Pido 1986, 62; Cariño 1987, 317). The greatest export of the Philippines became and continues to be its highly capable workforce, which provides a wide range of manual and intellectual service in dependent care, health care, business administration, hospitality, information technology, and engineering. Filipino medical and nursing care are world renowned. Filipinas are known for their competence and compassion as caregivers for children and the elderly (Magtalas 2004). By the end of the 1980s, researchers observed, "The overall picture of the effects of emigration on the Philippines is not very clear, but remittances seem to be important and there is evidence of substantial return migration and repatriation of earnings" (Fawcett and Cariño 1987, 19). Remittances to the Philippines by Filipino overseas workers in the Americas, Asia, Europe, and the Middle East, by some estimates, comprise 20–25 percent of the Philippine gross domestic product (GDP).

Their multicultural heritage, multilingual fluency (particularly in English), warm hospitality, and emphasis on smooth interpersonal relations have served Filipinos well in international institutions such as the World Bank, the United Nations, the Catholic Church, and transnational hotel and restaurant chains, as well as in hospitals, clinics, and medical centers around the world. They easily embody a cosmopolitan character and can adapt to different cultures on different continents. Given these characteristics and skills, as well as structural push factors in the Philippines, the Filipino diaspora will continue for the foreseeable future.

Diaspora in the United States

From the point of view of the United States with its British colonial history, immigration to the United States may be divided into four waves. Immigration experts Philip Martin and Elizabeth Midgley state:

> The first wave of immigrants arrived before entries began to be recorded in 1820. The English made up 60 percent of the population in 1790, but there were also Scots, Scots-Irish, Germans, and people from the Netherlands, France, and Spain. These migrants were motivated by a mixture of religious, political, and economic factors . . . The second wave of immigrants, who arrived between 1820 and 1860, fit well with the Americans' eagerness for people to help push back the frontier. Between 1820 and 1840, more than 750,000 German, British, and Irish immigrants arrived; another 4.3 million came from those countries during the next 20 years. About 40 percent were Irish escaping extreme poverty and famine in their home country. Roman Catholics predominated. The third wave of immigration started in 1880, when almost 460,000 immigrants arrived, and ended with the outbreak of war in Europe in 1914, when 1.2 million immigrants entered. During the third wave, over 20 million southern and eastern Europeans came, mostly to the eastern and Midwestern states. Chinese, Japanese and other Asian laborers settled in the western states . . . Fourth wave immigrants began arriving in the United States after 1965, when the preference system was changed. Instead of giving priority to immigrants based on their national origins, with preference to those from northern and Western Europe, the new system gave priority to people with U.S. relatives and to a small number of people with outstanding accomplishments or special skills. (Martin and Midgley 2003, 11–14)

These distinct waves, however, do not cover the migration of a small but critical mass of highly marketable Filipinos between 1946 and 1965. They were the first citizens of the newly independent Republic of the Philippines. Unlike the pioneer generation, they were not U.S. nationals. Like the pioneer generation, they too encouraged post-1965 immigration of family members. In addition to the World War II veterans and their families, a steady stream of such immigrants included Filipinos who joined the U.S. Navy in the Philippines

(Quinsaat 1976), and nurses and other health-care professionals recruited to work in U.S. hospital and medical facilities after the U.S. Information and Education Act established the Exchange Visitor program in 1948 (Choy 2003, 64). A sizable number of middle-class, second-generation Filipino Americans are the products of immigrant sailor and nurse marriages within established communities in San Diego, California; the San Francisco Bay Area; Oxon Hill, Maryland; and Virginia Beach, Virginia.

While an in-depth, systematic study of post-1965 Filipino immigrants to the United States has yet to be undertaken, it will be useful, as a background, to describe the experience of individual immigrants, reflecting both the middle and working classes.

THE POST-1965 MIDDLE-CLASS IMMIGRANTS

For these personal narratives, I chose my uncle, Eusebio Lucas Domingo, and my aunt, Casiana Pascual Lucas, both of whom actually wrote their autobiographies over the course of several weeks. They were well into their seventies when they wrote these personal histories. The first-person narrative in written or oral form remains rare in the Filipino-American community either as family story or community history. Yet it is a necessary element in giving a complete and accurate rendition of the ideas, values, knowledge, and experiences of Filipino Americans.

Casiana Pascual Lucas, Auntie Sianing, is my aunt by marriage to Uncle Lynn, Catalino Paguirigan Lucas, the youngest child of Eduardo Lucas and Basilisa Paguirigan and my mom's brother. Casiana was born on December 31, 1924, in Lihue, Kauai, to Zoilo Pascual and Liberata Salvador Paguyo. Her parents were among the hundreds of Filipino laborers who worked on the vast sugarcane plantations of Hawaii. Leaving most of their children in the Philippines, the Paguyos went to Kauai with their youngest child, three-year-old Rodolfo, and their nineteen-year-old son, Arcadio, who was able to work alongside his father on the plantations. Casiana and her younger brother, Cesar, were born in Hawaii. When Casiana was five, the family returned to the Philippines, although her dad and brother went back to Kauai shortly thereafter. Casiana's dad and brother returned from Kauai permanently when Casiana was about fifteen. She describes a middle-class childhood.

> My parents' sacrifices and hard work in Hawaii paid off because they were able to have a new house built for us in the Philippines. I felt comfortable living in our new beautiful home. When I was in my teens, I loved to plant and grow roses. I took pride displaying them on our window sills. I also liked to play records on the phonograph player that my father brought from Hawaii.[2]

When Auntie Sianing was sixteen, however, World War II broke out, disrupting not only one teenager's life but that of the entire Philippines, and indeed that of the entire world. Despite the hardships and aftermath of war, she was able to complete both high school and two years of college, earning a degree in elementary education. She also married my uncle, and they started their family. While Uncle Lynn was stationed in Manila with the Philippine Air Force, Auntie Sianing taught in the provinces for ten years. She raised my cousins with support from extended family and household help. Despite such large responsibilities, she managed to obtain a BS in education and to pass qualifying examinations to teach high school.

In 1959, Auntie Sianing, Uncle Lynn, and their children were reunited and lived for a time at Nichols Air Force Base, Pasay City. By 1966, however, they again were separated as Uncle Lynn migrated to the United States. They experienced homesickness, culture shock, family relationship adjustments, and financial difficulties like other immigrants before them. However, they persevered. Auntie Sianing was able to rise from file clerk to assistant underwriter for a major insurance company. Uncle Lynn left his department-store stock clerk position and joined my dad and uncles as a janitor and union member. This was not a professional occupation, but it was a working-class occupation with tenure, good wages, and benefits that provided steady income through retirement. My aunt and uncle were therefore able to send their children to college and watch them successfully participate in the labor force. Their two sons are U.S. Air Force retirees with second careers as an electrician and a radiology technician, respectively. Their daughters are nurses with administrative backgrounds who are married to physicians from non-Filipino backgrounds. In turn, among their grandchildren, several have graduated from college and entered the labor force, and the rest are counseled by their Grandma Sianing to pursue higher education and remember their Filipino heritage. Of course, she prays for all of them several times a day.

Eusebio Lucas Domingo is my mother's cousin. He was born on December 14, 1925, in Laoag, Ilocos Norte, Philippines, to Felix Domingo and Candida Lucas. His father was a general carpenter who had written an Ilocano novel even without a formal education. Uncle Sebio did not get to know his parents because his dad had gone to Hawaii to work in the sugar plantations, and he died right before Uncle Sebio was born. His mother died when he was three years old. He was raised by his maternal grandparents, Generoso and Macaria Lucas, in a distant barrio of Laoag, called Cawacawen, a rural farming area. Life was hard, but Uncle Sebio had a goal: "With all the ups and downs of life I went through, I was determined to follow the footsteps of my father. I have to study hard, go to distant places, and endeavor for a better life."[3] He did well in school as an honor student, an editor for his high-school paper, and the commanding officer of the Ilocos Norte High School Cadet Corps. He writes,

> My ambition was to become an electrical engineer, but due to the unavailability of financial support, I choose to become a military man. I joined the Philippine Army and rose to the ranks. While in the army, I took time to go to school. I finished my college education at the Far Eastern University in Manila with the degree of Bachelor of Science in Commerce, class 1959 . . . In 1948, I was a military student at the Ordnance School, Aberdeen Proving Grounds, Maryland, USA. I went to New York City for a tour.

Uncle Sebio also briefly describes enduring the hardships of World War II. He joined the 15th Infantry of the Philippine Army attached to the 205th Airborne Division of the U.S. 8th Army at Camp Spencer, Luna, La Union. After his stint he returned to Laoag to finish high school. He married his high-school sweetheart, Adoracion Fitelo, who became a high-school teacher and a UNESCO scholar at the Ateneo University of Manila. They led a comfortable, middle-class life and raised four daughters in the Philippines, yet chose to migrate to the United States in 1967. Today their children are employed in analytic, administrative, and customer-service positions in the military, health-care, and hospitality industries, mainly in the San Francisco Bay Area. Some of their grandchildren have already graduated from college and become gainfully employed. Uncle Sebio and Auntie Ador are leaders in their parish church and various organizations, including the Filipino Community of San Francisco and the Filipino Employees Association of PG&E Corporation. Now retired, they are members of Thousand Trails, a camping organization. When not babysitting their many grandchildren, they travel abroad and all over the United States in their motor home. Uncle Sebio notes,

> Although we have been enriched by American culture and tradition, we still observe our native Philippine values. My greatest joy is the successful achievements of my family in pursuing the great American Dream—the chance to enjoy a better and wholesome life in our new adopted country.

My aunt and uncle represent one group of post-1965 immigrants: those who were born to and experienced a hard life but were able to obtain a college education and lead a middle-class life in the Philippines before immigrating to the United States. They also possessed strong family values, ambition, and a sustained work ethic. This is not to say that everything was bliss. Generation gaps and the constant tension of good and evil have played out among the post-1965 immigrants and their children, just as among the pioneer generation and their children, grandchildren, and great-grandchildren. Filipino Americans, including the post-1965 immigrants, have had their share of such age-old sorrows as domestic violence, financial pressure, racial and national-origin discrimination, and disability and sickness. Nonetheless, the post-1965 immigrants with middle-class status in the Philippines were able to give their children and grandchildren access to the American Dream. They are responsible, in large part, for the relatively high socioeconomic status of Filipino Americans today. On the other hand, there is another group of post-1965 immigrants who were strictly working class in the Philippines and who, thus far, continue to be so in the United States.

POST-1965 DOMESTIC WORK IMMIGRANTS

There are two superimposed sets of Filipino-American communities. One is divided by the amount of time its members have been in the United States, and the other is divided by the class distinctions that its members developed in the Philippines. The former has to do with whether Filipino Americans see themselves as Americans of Filipino ancestry (the pioneer generation and their descendants) or as Filipinos in America (the post-1965 immigrants). The latter divide is between upper-class, professional Filipinos and Filipinos who are working-class domestic workers. The pre-1965 Filipino-American population was basically working class, so this earlier community was not divided by class. Those who were college educated were not necessarily employed in professional positions until after the 1965 Civil Rights Act, which forbade discrimination in employment by race, color, national origin, or creed. On the other hand, Filipinos in the Philippines were segregated by class and color. This caste system, particularly between the elite and working classes, including the servant class, was transferred to the United States with the post-1965 immigrants.

In the Washington, D.C., area, home to a substantial number of high-powered and high-earning multicultural families, various embassies, and international organizations, good domestic help is always in demand. In addition, there is a sizable mass of mainly white, well-to-do older people, with federal pensions or other retirement funds and investments, who seek companion care as they become less independent. Ever since I moved to the Washington, D.C., area in the 1970s, I have been approached by friends and strangers who ask me to recommend a good Filipino nanny or housekeeper because they know of the Filipinos' reputation for hard work, loving care, and proper demeanor. I was introduced to my first Filipino domestic worker in 1976 by a neighbor of my husband's parents. This neighbor was forever singing praises about how attentive and loving his Filipina cleaning lady was toward his elderly, infirm parents, and how everything sparkled and was kept in impeccable order by her. When we first met, she was bent over, cleaning the refrigerator. She was such a tiny thing, I thought she was a teenager. She was in her late thirties, a hard and savvy worker, looking for ways to supplement her less than minimum wage earnings by working long hours for a foreign diplomat. This was a story I would hear repeatedly as I got to know some of the Filipina domestic workers in the area over the next three decades (Lott 2003).

Often these domestic workers, almost all women, arrive in the United States as part of the household help of diplomats or employees of international organizations such as the World Bank. They do not always come directly from the Philippines. Sometimes they come via other Asian nations, Europe, or the Middle East, moving with their employers on their various assignments. Often they have gone to college and even have degrees. But they could not find jobs in the Philippines and so went abroad to help support their families. Like the pioneer generation before them, they send money back to the Philippines not only to help their parents and siblings but also to send their nieces and nephews to school. Through the years, some are able to obtain green cards with their employer's sponsorship. This is no small accomplishment given the long wait for green-card applicants from the Philippines, a wait that can easily stretch to decades. In addition to their primary jobs, they hold several part-time jobs—cleaning houses, catering Filipino food such as lumpia,[4] serving at formal international receptions, selling cosmetics or insurance, being a nanny, or providing companionship and care to single seniors. They need more than one job to make ends meet due to the low wages of domestic workers and minimal, if any, benefits. Yet they provide critical skills, especially in terms of human care. Many are frugal in their long-term plans. Some make investments in real estate in the Philippines and the United States, sometimes by building what they envision will be their retirement homes. They have an extensive network, keeping each other informed of jobs, reasonably priced apartments, social gatherings, and changes in employment and immigration policies. Like the pioneer generation, they continue the chain of migration. Because of the careful attention they pay to the bureaucratic process and to their financial savings, several domestic workers are now, upon attaining U.S. permanent residence and citizenship, beginning to sponsor their children, parents, and siblings. At this point, it is not clear what their future will be in the United States, as some decide to stay, while others return or are returned by their sponsors to the Philippines.

The success of the working and professional classes of Filipino immigrants, like that of immigrants before them, is due in part to their being risk-takers, hard workers, optimists, and survivors. On the other hand, just as with the pioneer generation after the Great Depression and World War II, the self-help efforts of the post-1965 immigrants are complemented by beneficial U.S. policies and programs directed toward a common destiny. Although my father's generation also were in lower-paid and lower-status occupations, they had the benefit of union membership when the labor movement was a major institutional power. (As I've noted, unions blocked the membership of racial and ethic minorities, but some gradually included them, even as officers.) Domestic workers in 2005, which are made up disproportionately of racial and ethnic minorities and women, including Filipino-American women, have minimal, if any, collective bargaining power.

STRATEGIC ENTRY INTO THE UNITED STATES
IN THE POST–CIVIL RIGHTS ERA

The law of unintended consequences plays out repeatedly in the realm of public policy. For example, although the 1965 immigration amendments increased the entry of Asians into the United States, no one could project the tremendous increase in the U.S. Asian population in the subsequent decades. In the 1960 U.S. Census there were only about 1 million Asians in contrast to 178 million whites. By the 1980 U.S. Census, due to liberal use of chain migration, the U.S. Asian population had almost quadrupled to 3.7 million. Similarly, under equal employment opportunity laws and an expanding economy, American women entered the work force in great numbers in the 1970s and 1980s and assumed many traditionally male-occupied, higher-paid positions. Although women were entering occupations that had not been open to women traditionally, these positions did not necessarily continue to be highly paid positions. Women attained close to equal pay with men not because they increased their earnings relative to men but because American men's earnings started to decline in 1973. By the 1990s, dual-income households were required if Americans wished to acquire the same standard of living attained by a one-earner middle-class (mainly white) household in the 1950s.

The law of unintended consequences for Filipino Americans and other racial minorities, particularly blacks who were at the forefront of the civil rights movement, was to see these hard-won civil rights for historically disadvantaged minorities extended to new settlers who had not grown up in a racially segregated United States. At first, this was not problematic. Over time, however, the number and proportion of new settlers of color became greater than those of some groups of longtime residents, including Filipinos. Moreover, the new immigrants did not necessarily share the worldview or priorities of their U.S.-born kin, given their different experiences, histories, and positions of power.

Second-generation Filipinos have described this dissonance between post-1965 immigrants and the U.S history of racial segregation.

Unlike Bulosan and his peers, they do not come to a land that permits legal discrimination. Unlike Bulosan's generation, many of the newcomers are highly educated. Unlike my generation, many have not raised their families in racially segregated, economically disadvantaged neighborhoods. Unlike the first two
generations, many profess never to have felt the sting of racism. (Bacho 1997, 8)

The newly arrived immigrant Filipinos did not personally relate to the history of
exclusion experienced by earlier generations of Filipino Americans. Access to
jobs, housing, and education was now legally ensured for these new Americans,
thanks in part to the civil rights and anti-discrimination efforts of groups such as
FAYTS. Moreover, the priorities of the new immigrants were still rooted in the
motherland. Unlike FAYTS, their energies went to assisting relatives abroad and
in supporting the anti-Marcos movement. (Jamero 1997, 313)

Like the members of other racial minorities who were historically disadvantaged, working-class Americans of Filipino ancestry watched as middle-class,
college-educated post-1965 immigrants and their children benefited not only
from nondiscrimination but from affirmative action, particularly in higher education and professional employment. They understood clearly that,

Within the United States, the civil rights and feminist movements reframed the
American notions of social membership, economic opportunities, equality, and
assimilation. Today's migrants thus enter a society transformed by the expansion
of opportunities for minority group members and women and also by patterns of
industrial restructuring that have drastically altered the economic environment.
(Foner, Rumbaut, and Gold 2000)

On the other hand, sociologist Antonio Pido, a post-1965 immigrant who ob-
tained his doctorate from Michigan State University in 1976, provides another view,

In contrast to such American-born Pilipinos, the new "brain drain" type of immigrants often had a very good idea of the racial issues in the United States before they immigrated. They were more aware that they were not coming to the
land of equal opportunity, at least between the races. They hoped that the im-
provements in civil rights in the United States and their educational and occupational credentials would place them on a better footing than the earlier immigrants. They are conscious of being nonwhite immigrants in a white-dominated
society. From being a racial majority in the Philippines, they have become a
racial minority among competing minorities. This puts them in an uncomfort-
able position in dealing with the majority and with other minority groups.
    For example, many are not completely informed about and are sometimes
ambivalent about affirmative action. On the basis of the inaccurate but popular
perception that unqualified minorities and women can get jobs and promotions
only by affirmative action, they feel that they do not need affirmative action be-

cause many are overqualified for many jobs. The perception is further based on the assumption of a real equality of opportunity or a "level playing field" . . .
. . . At the same time, some sympathize with other minorities who have been and continue to be deprived. They are often faced with a clash of perspectives. As individuals, they are qualified or even overqualified for the jobs they apply for or have. But as immigrants, do they have rights to jobs that other "true Americans" fought so hard for, only to have taken from them by later arrivals to this country? The situation is exacerbated by subtle and not-so-subtle attempts to pit them and other Asians (i.e., "model minorities") against blacks, Hispanics, and Native Americans. (Pido 1997, 33–34)

In all fairness, while some new arrivals did not identify themselves as part of a racial minority, many of the post-1965 immigrants continued the struggle against racial discrimination, including discrimination based on accent. Some post-1965 immigrants experienced racial discrimination similar but not equal to that experienced by earlier Filipino Americans. For example, the two groups were similar in their opposition to job discrimination on the basis of race. They were different in that this job discrimination was in terms of professional rather than manual-labor occupations. To take one specific example, in 1974 Purisima Salazar, a registered nurse, won her suit against Blue Shield of California for promotion discrimination. The settlement required Blue Shield of California to award Mrs. Salazar unpaid compensation and lost benefits. In addition, Blue Shield was required to set up a forty-thousand-dollar claim fund for back pay to Asian Americans who believed that they had suffered discrimination in promotion (*San Francisco Examiner* January 3, 1975, 3). Mrs. Salazar was supported in her suit by United Pilipinos for Equal Employment, a community affirmative action group founded in March 1973.

The post-1965 immigrants' sense of injustice as a racial minority was accompanied by a grave awareness of human rights, given their years under martial law, and because they had seen the mistreatment of Filipino overseas workers and had witnessed the People Power Revolution of 1986 that ended the Marcos regime. How would the inclusion of Philippine citizens with a strong sense of nationalism and a record of human-rights awareness mesh with the social order of American citizens of Filipino ancestry?

THE SOCIAL ORDER: EXPATRIATES OR U.S. CITIZENS?

For centuries, a common theme of the immigrant story has been a longing for the life left behind while adjusting to the new one. Adults more so than children struggle with this change. As shown by studies of immigrant youth (Portes 1996), children can more easily navigate in their new land than can their parents. The pioneer generation were mainly young men, a good portion of whom were teenagers whose allegiance was still in formation. Besides, as schoolchildren they had pledged their allegiance to the United States. They were not Philippine citizens but U.S. nationals. Their U.S.-born children then were American citizens. In contrast, the post-1965 immigrants were expatriates. They and their children who immigrated with them were citizens of the Philippines.

Where Do the "Ex-Pats" Fit In?

In various Filipino-American media, such as *Filipinas* magazine, Philippine expatriates are called "ex-pats." The content of such media, published primarily by post-1965 immigrants, largely focuses on events and personalities in the Philippines. While some of these media, such as *Filipinas*, are conscientious about covering news of the United States and of Americans of Filipino ancestry, the target audience is more one of Filipino expatriates than of U.S. citizens. In his seminal study *The Pilipinos in America*, Antonio Pido reminds us that the love of country of the Filipinos is based on culture.

> The loyalty of the Pilipino immigrant to the Philippines is based primarily on the cultural heritage rather than the nation state. Literature, the arts, music and food that are Pilipino are valued as those aspects of Philippine culture that give more meaning to life: smooth interpersonal relationships; long-lasting and nonutilitarian interpersonal relationships; the value of reciprocity; and respect and concern for the old. Identity concerns of the Pilipino center on how these values may be maintained while allowing the pursuance of economic goals. Pilipinos are proud to be American citizens, especially when they are in the Philippines. However, they are also proud of their Philippine cultural heritage. (Pido 1986, 123)

By contrast, the identity of American citizens, including Filipino Americans and other racial minorities, stems from the Constitution and the mutual rights and responsibilities of representative government and individual residents and citizens.

Pido goes on to say that the post-1965 immigrants came to the United States not just for the opportunities in America but also because in their calculus they often reluctantly concluded that the Philippines did not provide long-term opportunities for them.

> Given the constraints of both the Philippines and the U.S., Pilipino immigrants believed that the United States offered better chances for pursuing what they perceived to be meaningful lives as human beings. This study has shown that another choice for many immigrants was between control by the values, norms, and social structure of the Philippines vis-à-vis more individual autonomy elsewhere. Social and geographic distance from the cultural, social, and structural

constraints in the Philippines, combined with their perceptions of the U.S. values and structures allowing maximum individual autonomy, made them prefer the latter. (Pido 1986, 122)

For the "ex-pats," the familiar social order of the Philippines was replaced by a post–World II and post–civil rights movement American social order. This order reflected the end of racial segregation, the start of racial integration, and an environment of equal opportunity. As they adjusted to this new order, the expatriates carried with them the vestiges of the Philippine one. At times they seemed to have dual allegiances, both simultaneously and alternatively.

Dual Allegiance

For the pioneer generation and their children, their defining moments, as with other Americans, included the assassination of President John F. Kennedy and the Vietnam War. For the post-1965 immigrants, their defining moments were inevitably martial law under Ferdinand Marcos and the assassination of Benigno Aquino that fueled the 1986 People Power Revolution. In the 1970s, as the pioneer generation and their children focused on the Vietnam War and the U.S. domestic agenda, the post-1965 immigrants would insist on suspension of martial law as the priority of any community agenda. There were visible and painful splits between Filipino Americans and Filipinos in America. Moreover, the post-1965 immigrants were divided among themselves into pro-Marcos and anti-Marcos factions. The pioneer generation and their children, while sympathetic to the newcomers' concerns, sought to focus their energies on American issues. These differences continued through the 1980s, 1990s, and 2000s. Even in the writings of expatriates today (in *Filipinas*, for example), the focus is on their past and present in the Philippines more than on their future in the United States or even in the Philippines.

It is not unusual for formal gatherings and business meetings of expatriates to include renditions of both the Philippine and American national anthems. The expatriates have representatives of the Philippine Embassy or consulates partake in their community deliberations. They strategize and jockey to be representatives of both the United States and the Philippines in politics and business. Some seem to be biding their time in the United States until the opportunity comes for them to return to the Philippines to assume positions of power. They link American issues with Philippine ones, such as in the effort to obtain benefits for Filipino veterans of World War II in the Philippine military similar to those of Filipino-American veterans who served in the U.S. military. The ability of the larger Filipino-American community to engage fully in American democracy is sometimes overshadowed by the expatriates' confounding of Philippine issues with Filipino-American ones. Whereas the pioneer and second generations have focused on public issues within the institutional process and are comfortable with multicultural coalitions, expatriates tend to focus to a greater extent on parochial issues while using the process of interpersonal relations, such as the *compadre* (godfather) system. The continuing immigration of Filipinos to the United States assures continuous allegiance to a Philippine agenda. What remains to be seen is how this dual allegiance will relate to the dual citizenship of the expatriates. The Citizenship Retention and Re-Acquisition Act of 2003, also known as the dual citizenship law, enabled native-born Filipinos who had become U.S. citizens to reacquire their Philippine citizenship (Guerrero 2003). While it remains to be seen whether Filipino Americans born in the Philippines who have become U.S. citizens will choose to be dual citizens, dual allegiance can become problematic, given transnational economies and very easy travel and communications, for personal, economic, and political reasons. Nevertheless, the expatriates' children are becoming more American. Will their allegiance, more and more, gravitate to the United States, like that of the children of immigrants before them?

A SECOND, SECOND GENERATION

Immigration researchers are now studying the "new second generation" (Portes 1996). These are basically the children of the post-1965 immigrants. These researchers pose the same question that Filipino-American parents ask: "Will my children be able to achieve the American Dream as did the children of European immigrants, or will they be systematically blocked from achievement as were children of color in the United States historically?" Portes, however, frames the issue somewhat differently.

> Today's second generation finds itself somewhere in between these extremes. Its members confront the same reduced circumstances in the American labor market affecting domestic minorities. Most second generation youth are also nonwhite and hence subject to the same discrimination endured by their predecessors (Jensen 1990; Passel and Edmonston 1992). On the other hand, immigrant families and communities commonly possess material and moral resources that confer advantages on their young as they seek avenues for successful adaptation. In the new "hourglass" economy shaped by the industrial restructuring of the American labor market, the path toward economic success consists of traversing the narrowing "middle" between dead-end menial jobs at the bottom and the growing pool of managerial and professional occupations requiring advanced degrees at the top. (Portes 1996, 5)

Portes cautions that,

> The second generation is the key to establishing the long-term consequences of immigration, but the course of its adaptation is uncertain at present. The ques-

tions of shifts in language and ethnic identities are part of a more general puzzle. This puzzle is whether today's children of immigrants will follow their European predecessors and move steadily into the middle class mainstream or whether, on the contrary, their ascent will be blocked and they will join children of earlier black and Puerto Rican migrants as part of an expanded multiethnic underclass. As the deteriorating conditions of life in American cities suggest, the question is of more than passing significance for the future of American society. (Portes 1996, 3)

I see this situation as an example of whether common destiny will prevail over Manifest Destiny. It is not only the new second generation but all American children who must face the "hourglass economy." Already there is talk of the increasing divide between the "haves" and "have-nots," between the winners and losers in the new economy. How will America's future generations fare? One strength of immigrant communities noted by researchers lies in their "ability to call co-ethnics to reinforce normative expectations vis-à-vis their offspring and to supervise their behavior" (Portes 1995, 257). On the other hand Portes notes that, "This type of social capital dissipates when communities become less cohesive."

While this situation is a topic of conversation among many post-1965 immigrants, including those Filipino Americans who are worried about their children and grandchildren forgetting their heritage and traditions, this concern is expressed by many Americans of various generations. Some U.S.-born Americans also recount, with nostalgia, the not-too-distant past in which Americans grew up in communities where all the children were protected and nurtured by their neighbors, particularly in nonurban areas. This was before the rise of the postindustrial economy that triggered the tremendous movement of U.S. women into the labor force. Now with many U.S. families either dual-earner or single-parent households, children spend less time with their parents or with extended-family adults. While a sizable proportion of the second-generation children and grandchildren of Auntie Sianing and Uncle Sebio and their peers achieved the American Dream, they also encountered the structural conditions and barriers that contribute to the breakup of families and communities, conditions that include domestic violence, divorce, substance abuse, and decreased civic participation. For example, at the national conference of the Filipino American Women's Network held in San Mateo, California, in 2000, there was much joy in celebrating the accomplishments of multigenerational Filipino women. Yet there was also great surprise, sadness, and even denial when attendees were confronted with research findings indicating that young Filipina-American women (in their late teens and twenties) had a growing rate of suicide. The future of America's children, both native and immigrant, is intertwined. Similarly, the offspring of the pioneer generation and the post-1965 immigrants are parts of a greater whole.

DIFFERENCES BETWEEN THE PIONEER AND SECOND
GENERATIONS AND THE POST-1965 IMMIGRANTS

Yet even with the continuous arrival of Filipinos to the United States each year, the differences between the earlier, settled population of Filipino Americans and the post-1965 Filipinos are not as great as their similarities. The initial, visible differences were along the lines of working- or middle-class affiliation; the possession or lack of a college education; Ilocano-Visayan or Tagalog background; rural or urban orientation; pro- or anti-Marcos political sympathy; and multicultural or ethnocentric outlook. A more subtle difference lay in the fact that the Filipino emphasis on smooth interpersonal relationships, which was practiced by expatriates, stood in contrast to the direct, sometimes adversarial, style of American interpersonal relationships exhibited by the second and later generations. Oftentimes, expatriates view Filipino-American children, including their own, as not as respectful and well-behaved as Filipino children. Pido notes that smooth interpersonal relations and behavior can be an asset.

> The traditional Pilipino pattern of interpersonal behavior relating to avoidance of interpersonal friction has served the Pilipino immigrant well in adjusting to a new culture. This helped him balance perceived needs while maintaining some cultural integrity. Cultural integrity can be asserted when needed, but it can also be suspended when necessity demands. (Pido 1985, 123)

The greatest difference between these earlier and later groups, however, is in the length of time they have been in the United States and in their attachment to the Philippines. Expatriates primarily identify themselves as Filipinos in America, whereas the pioneer generation and their descendants view themselves as Americans of Filipino ancestry. Members of the pioneer generation acknowledge their Filipino identity, but they have a multiplicity of identities consistent with the American emphasis on the individual rather than on the individual's group membership.

COMMON GROUND

Regardless of their differences, the pioneer generation and the post-1965 immigrants are permanent settlers in the United States. Many are or will be American citizens, just like their offspring. They are here to partake in the rights and responsibilities of American citizenship. Like their parents, the younger generations are called to defend the freedoms of this nation as a representative democracy and to contribute to its prosperity as a capitalistic economy. In addition, they contribute to the United States their Philippine legacy of acceptance of family and generational relationships and responsibilities, an appreciation for smooth interpersonal relationships, and a concern for those less fortunate. They are part of the future of the United States. This understanding of the perhaps unique, value-added role of Filipino Americans to the future of the United States is important as Americans again reassess who and what an American is and renegotiate the social contract between the U.S. government and all residents of the United States, as well as between the United States and its fellow nations. The United States is at a critical historical junction as it is again faced with tensions between Manifest Destiny and common destiny that will have a global impact.

In spite of their differences, the two segments of the Filipino-American population described above have already begun to overlap and even blur as marriages and family formation occur between U.S.-born Filipino Americans and the immigrants. The Filipino-American population itself is at a critical juncture and a potentially strategic position. It is maturing and coming into its own. It is the second-largest Asian-American population in the United States, after the Chinese. The pioneer generation and the post-1965 immigrant generation are both raising the next generation. These multigenerational Filipino Americans are in the forefront, along with other Asian Americans and Hispanics, of the struggle to change the future social order of the United States from a white-black hierarchy to a new civic order beyond race and color stratification and the other ascribed characteristics used to subjugate and exclude minority Americans from their full rights, responsibilities, and opportunities as U.S. residents and citizens.

This new stage of Filipino-American history is captured by Pido.

> Pilipino Americans are now more conscious and assertive of their place and rights in the United States. The civil rights movement also brought new civil and voting rights laws. The youth perceive themselves as legitimate members of the American household, with the same rights and privileges as other Americans. But whatever their emotional allegiance to their ethnicity and culture, it does not prevent them from full participation in America . . .
>
> . . . There are virtually no Pilipino or Asian publications in the United States that do not have news items on the "first" Pilipino (or other Asian) who is appointed or elected to a position at the local, state, or national level in government, a corporation, or nonprofit organization. These people did not achieve this recognition merely by the support of fellow ethnics, but rather by the support of a multicultural community. Such solidarity did not happen to the Pilipino Americans because they are Pilipinos who are in America, as their parents and grandparents were, but rather because they are Americans who are Pilipinos. (Pido 1997, 36–37)

The post-1965 immigrants are a distinct segment of the Filipino American population. They made and continue to make the adjustment from a racial majority in the Philippines to a racial minority in the United States. Like most immigrants before them, they come to the United States for opportunity and freedom. Many of them hold graduate and professional degrees and bring highly marketable skills to the United States as professionals. Other post-1965 immigrants may range from being no more than high-school graduates to having some college education. They also possess highly marketable skills that support the service industries, particularly human-care and health-care industries. Both groups have a familiarity with American culture and a degree of English-language fluency. Despite their dual allegiance to the Philippines and the United States, they and their children are here to stay. Together with the pioneer generation, they are the grandparents and great-grandparents to multicultural and multiracial Filipino Americans of the twenty-first century.

NOTES

1. According to Rimonte, the term *hidalgo*, meaning "son of God," is of Arabic origin but was used by Spaniards to differentiate themselves from colonized inferiors, including Filipinos. "This conviction of innate nobility that marked him as intrinsically superior to everyone is related to the famous Spanish indolence and parasitism, about which much has been written (Ellis 1920; Roth, 1974)" (Rimonte 1997, 43).

2. From the unpublished autobiography of Casiana Pascual Lucas as dictated to and transcribed by her daughter, Myrna Lucas Fleming, over several months in 2002 and 2003.

3. Excerpted from the unpublished autobiography of Eusebio Lucas Domingo.

4. Filipino version of an Asian spring roll.

Chapter Five

Fast-Food Take-Out: Multicultural/Multiracial Children, Grandchildren, and Great-Grandchildren

Well, son, I'll tell you:
Life for me ain't been no crystal stair.
It's had tacks in it,
And splinters,
And boards torn up,
And places with no carpet on the floor—
Bare.
But all the time
I'se been a-climbin' on,
And reachin' landin's,
And turnin' corners,
And sometimes goin' in the dark
Where there ain't been no light.
So boy, don't you turn back.
Don't you set down on the steps
'Cause you finds it's kinder hard.
Don't you fall now—
For I'se still goin', honey,
I'se still climbin',
And life for me ain't been no crystal stair.

—Langston Hughes, "Mother to Son"

Just like the pioneer and post-1965 immigrant generations of Filipinos who came to America left their parents' homes by sea and sky, the second generation has spread its wings across the United States and even other nations. Those who opted for careers with the U.S. armed forces can be found in different stations around the world. Those who opted for graduate training and professional careers left home for Ivy League and other campuses. Upon completion of training, some returned home to Seattle, Washington, or

Vallejo, California, or Pearl City, Hawaii, but many did not. Multigenerational reunions can be quite a logistical feat. While this is not uncommon for an increasingly mobile U.S. population, Filipino Americans are distinguished by a greater proportion of multicultural and multiracial families, larger families that are in keeping with their Catholic tradition and child-oriented culture, and the continuing inclusion and presence of extended-family members at their gatherings. In addition, Filipinos and Filipino Americans are tolerant of the diversity of their family members. For example, children born out of wedlock are commonly acknowledged and treated as part of the family. Also, Filipinos are more open to "tomboy love" or the *bakla*, that is, Filipino and Filipino-American homosexuals. While these members of Filipino and Filipino-American families have existed for generations, it is only recently that necessary research on this population has begun. *Filipinas* has published thoughtful narratives of this segment of the Filipino and Filipino-American populations. One example is a poignant article by Marites N. Sison on the same-sex relationships of some domestic workers who must leave their families and loved ones to earn their livelihood and remit wages to support their families (2004, 54–55). Such stories are poignant because many Filipino domestic workers, whether heterosexual or homosexual, are caregivers who give not only their care but also their love and affection to so many others outside their own families (Lott 2002, 54–55).

Christmastime at the Tamayo-Lucas family homes with Lola Anicia Tamayo and Lola Casiana Lucas presiding is always a kaleidoscopic affair. Their children-in-law are Filipino immigrants, Korean immigrants, Chinese Americans, blacks, and whites. Their grandchildren are every color of the rainbow. Their grandchildren-in-law are Samoan, Chinese, Burmese, and Filipino American thus far. When my mom and aunt compare notes with their cousins and Filipino friends, they find they all have a rainbow of children-in-law, grandchildren, and great-grandchildren. Their holiday dinner tables are a smorgasbord showcasing my mom's fried chicken and my aunt's *lumpia*; my cousin Nestor's Chinese sweet-and-sour spareribs; Tagalog fish and seafood soup; Asian bitter greens with tomatoes and onions; down-home *pinakbet*;[1] several kinds of seaweed and bamboo-shoot salads; fiesta *lechon*;[2] marinated grilled skewers of beef and chicken; and other Filipino dishes, many made by their immigrant Filipino children-in-law. Desserts cover the side buffet: Chinese sponge cake; American cheesecake; my sister-in-law Debbie's apple pie; freshly sliced mango and pineapple; chocolates; and three flavors of ice cream with whipped cream and sprinkles. The grandmothers fret that everyone can't show up for these multigenerational celebrations and, if they do, they all come at different times. My cousins and their spouses are in the health-care field, working different shifts at various hospitals. And of course, many of our children are young adults with their own schedules. In addition to the holiday season, we have many December birthdays. My aunt's and mother's birthdays fall between Christmas and New Year's Day. My cousin Carol's birthday falls on the day after Christmas, and my brother-in-law, Fante, is a New Year's Day baby. One year we were all just partied out, and instead of making these homemade dinners, we ended up celebrating my mom's birthday with carryout pizza and sushi. Everyone ate well. Needless to say, our children, and now even fourth-generation Nicholas, know how to party, play, and get along with multicultural, multiple generations under many conditions. They've learned to be open and receptive to all kinds of cuisines and forms of hospitality as well as to help out in serving large crowds. My cousins, siblings, and I wonder how many more multigenerational gatherings will occur—and who will host them—as we watch our children bring in french fries and milkshakes from the neighborhood fast-food restaurant.

This chapter on the third and fourth generations of Filipino Americans is a chapter in progress. That is, while there is a body of historical fact, immigrant theory, statistics, literature, autobiography, and biography describing prior American generations, the lives of Generation X , the millennial generation, and the digital generation, including their specific Filipino-American counterparts, are still unfolding. While the silent and baby boom generations (which would include me) may examine, analyze, describe, and speculate about these younger generations, such commentary is incomplete and may even be inaccurate. It is incomplete because it is the commentary of outsiders. Commentary by older generations may be inaccurate because the conventional assumption of past generations—that they are first children and then parents in order to ensure continuing generations and the survival of the species—may not necessarily be shared by or be the trajectory for present and future generations. Most important, these younger generations have not yet reached their prime. In the fluid and quick pace of the first decade of the twenty-first century there is time to anticipate many changes but not enough, perhaps, to foresee lasting trends.

The demographic reality is that negative, that is, below-replacement fertility rates are true of Japan and many postindustrial Western European nations. The United States may very well follow that trend, or not. Additionally, the rate of children born to single women and the rate of couples living together outside of marriage are increasing in postindustrial nations. Whereas in the mid-1960s Senator Daniel Moynihan, then a Department of Labor official, noted that almost one-third of black children were born to single women, today one-third of all U.S. children are born to single women. The rate in some Western European nations is about one half. Although this varies by race, origin, income, and education, the trend in the United States is troubling. Moreover, the U.S. divorce rate for first marriages still hovers at 50 percent. These demographic trends challenge the continuation of families and multiple generations in which adults formally and collectively are responsible for children. Will these trends exist for the grandchildren and great-grandchildren of the Filipino pioneer generation, the post-1965 immigrants, and their descendants?

These trends are also occurring in a major new stage of the American economy and democratic republic. Just as the expansions of the agricultural and industrial eras in the United States sharpened the tensions and conflicts between Manifest Destiny and common destiny, the global reach of the information era in the twenty-first century will also provide new manifestations of Manifest Destiny and common destiny for Filipino American and other American grandchildren and great-grandchildren. The timeless issues of group competition, division of labor, and the ownership and allocation of sustainable resources are accompanied by the unique question of individuals who may be part of or in solidarity with many social groups or are not a member of any group. While there have always been a few individuals who prize their solitude, the United States now has a critical mass of individuals per se, with single-person households continuing to increase proportionally and numerically. Persons who expected to be grandparents are not. Persons who expected to be parents are not. Persons who choose to delay childbearing may or may not become parents.

THE DECISION TO HAVE CHILDREN

This decision is governed by many influences. Having children satisfies a primal need. And our parents who had fought World War II were thankful to have peace restored and to be able to start families, hence the baby boomers. Much of animal, including human, history can be viewed as elders bearing and nurturing their young, even if their own lives are at stake. Until the twentieth century, mothers dying during child-birth was not uncommon, and this remains true for many mothers in the Third World today. On one hand, adults, particularly parents, are expected to sacrifice and make commitments for the next generation, and having children has often historically been a given or a duty. On the other hand, a sizable number of births are accidents.

Reproductive Choice and the Subtle Revolution

Among my fellow baby boomers, however, the decision for procreation was raised to a new level with our ability to control more effectively the "right" conditions for when and how to have a baby. That is, the decision to be or not to be a parent was beginning to be viewed as an individual choice. Reproductive choice was fought for by the silent and baby boom generations all the way to the Supreme Court 1973 decision of *Roe v. Wade*. Subsequent generations of U.S. women, including the third and fourth generations of Filipino Americans, now see reproduction as a choice. This assumption is not a given to be taken for granted, however, as many younger generations of American women are discovering.

This visibly radical departure from earlier views of procreation was accompanied by a slower, multidecade change termed the "subtle revolution" by Ralph E. Smith. In 1979, Smith wrote,

> The movement of women into the paid labor force is a revolution in the sense that it is bringing about a fundamental change in social and economic conditions. The division of labor between the sexes in which men work outside the home for pay while women engage in unpaid housework is breaking down. And, as more women work outside the home, the fight for equal treatment in the job market and equal responsibilities for unpaid domestic work has intensified. Indeed, female-male relationships in every aspect of society are being questioned and are changing . . . But the revolution's association with women's movement into the paid labor force is, in many ways, a subtle revolution. It is subtle in that it has been gradual, not traceable to any abrupt change. Decade after decade, the percentage of the female population in the labor force (that is, women's participation rate) has been increasing. Since 1947, when statistics began to be collected on a regular basis, the participation rate of women has increased in all but four years. (Smith 1979, 1–2)

As previously mentioned, the labor-force participation rates of Filipino and Filipino-American women has historically been high. Work outside the home for pay, however, has not precluded Filipino and Filipino-American women from being spouses and parents, often in households with a greater number of children than the average American family. The care and upbringing of children by parents and extended-family members have always been a priority for multiple generations of Filipino Americans. Even within these parameters, however, there is variation across generations on when to have children, how to care for them, and who will care for them.

Roni and Fante, Nita and Rob, Bill and Debbie, Greg and Cass

My sister, Roni, and my brother-in-law, Fante, are members of the silent generation. They graduated from college and had full-time jobs for several years before they married in 1971. Their older child, Gregory, was born the following year. Their younger child, Allan, followed after six years. Roni and Fante chose to continue full-time work with two brief maternity leaves for Roni. In the 1970s, their infant and preschool care included split work shifts, grandparents, family friends, and the child-care center at Fante's work site. In the 1980s, after-school care was provided by a neighbor, with Grandma as emergency backup. This combination of arrangements was not an unusual arrangement for many Filipino-American families, who preferred care by grandparents, especially grandmothers not in the labor force.

In contrast to Roni and Fante, my husband, Rob, and I married right out of graduate school. As baby boomers, we were comfortable leading a childfree life for several years. After seven years of marriage and work, to my mother's relief, our older child, David, was born. I opted to return to full-time work after three months of maternity leave. For six months, my son had a caregiver in our home. When he was nine months old, my mother-in-law cared for David. When David was fifteen months old, Joseph, our younger child, was born. With two babies, I took six months of maternity leave, planning to return to the full-time labor force because I had by that point reached a senior management level. In the early 1980s, senior management positions were still a rarity for women, especially young women and women of color. I had three options: to return to paid work full time, to return to paid work part time, or to be a full-time, stay-at-home mom. For various reasons, I chose the last option. This form of child care allowed me, among other things, to play with my children, and even to organize spontaneous picnics at the National Zoo on their father's lunch hour. I also honed useful life skills during this period by helping kindergarteners learn to read; testifying with mixed success before a board of education in an attempt to prevent the cutting of budgets for gym and music classes, and advanced math and sciences courses; chairing Boy Scout troop committee meetings; and learning how to tie life-saving knots. As my children entered school in the mid-1980s, I developed a home-based consulting business using a personal computer, modem, and fax machine. I reentered the full-time labor force when David was a senior in high school in 1997.

My brother, Bill, and my sister-in-law, Debbie, as younger baby boomers, took yet a different course, and one that is more common among some dual-income families of the 1990s and 2000s. After college graduation, they devoted time to their careers and interests before marrying in their thirties. Their older child, Araceli, was born before their third wedding anniversary. Their younger child, Lorenzo, was born when his sister was seven years old. Debbie took maternity leave, and Bill also used family leave based on the federal Family and Medical Leave Act. Infant care was provided at home by a caregiver shared with another family. Preschool care was provided by a private nursery, again with Grandma as emergency backup. After-school care is at a child-care center.

On December 18, 2000, my nephew, Greg, and niece-in-law, Cass, became parents to Nicholas, the first member of the fourth generation of the Tamayo-Lucas family and the first great-grandchild of Lazaro and Anicia. Greg and Cass are a part of Generation X, having graduated from San Jose State in the mid-1990s and ridden the roller coaster of Silicon Valley for almost a decade when they were in their twenties. Cass also took maternity leave to care for

Nicholas. Shortly after her return to work in 2001, her position was eliminated. She eventually found another job. During her job search, Nicholas was enrolled in an infant and toddler child-care center. He is currently in an all-day nursery school with backup care from Greg, who is currently working as a home-based consultant. Care by Nicholas's maternal and paternal grandparents is problematic because they live in separate cities and are still in the paid labor force.

These examples suggest a couple of conclusions on the present and future care for children in the United States. First, child care in 2005 is increasingly provided outside the family via all sorts of arrangements. This is partly due to greater and longer labor-force participation by parents, coupled with the decreasing availability of extended-family assistance for child care. Second, adults are constantly balancing their paid-work and family responsibilities. This is particularly true for single-parent households and parents who must work at more than one job. Commutes are longer and cover greater distances. Moreover, in a global information economy, national and even international travel for business is not uncommon. Electronic communications ensure a 24-7 economy, further eroding the boundaries between family time and work-force time.

In one sense, the opportunity and choice that we have been given to be individuals as well as family members is consistent with the American founding settlers' Declaration of Independence and succeeding generations' dream of being free to achieve their full potential. U.S. residents and citizens today are beneficiaries of statutes and policies related to equality. Ascribed characteristics, notably race, national origin and sex, can no longer be the legal basis for stratification and exclusion. Employment and educational opportunities are available to those who have marketable skills in the global economy. The nation's growing multiracial-multicultural background, its above-average incomes, and the above-average educational achievements of the offspring of the pioneer and following generations may mean a common destiny of equality and freedom for all future generations of Americans. The pioneer generation marvels at the opportunities for life, liberty, and the pursuit of happiness available to their offspring. On the other hand, they acknowledge that the younger generations of the twenty-first century may face their own versions of Manifest Destiny. How these younger generations transform Manifest Destiny into common destiny remains to be seen, but they are poised to play a critical role in such a transformation.

THE MILLENNIAL GENERATION—
THE CLASS OF 2000 AND BEYOND

In understanding the grandchildren and great-grandchildren of the pioneer generation, it is not sufficient to discuss them as third- and fourth-generation

Filipino Americans. It is also necessary to understand the American context in which they have grown up and prepared for adulthood. This section focuses primarily on the millennial generation, but it also considers the smaller cohorts that preceded them, namely, Generation X and the digital generation that followed it. While the 1970s are noted for decreasing school enrollment, this trend was reversed by the end of the 1980s. The growth in school-age population has continued through 2004. Two reasons for this change were the increased immigration of populations of childbearing age, many of whom wanted their children to be educated in the United States, and baby boomers whose nesting instincts had been put on hold as they pursued individual interests. The boomers found their biological clocks ticking away, however, and turned their attention to creating families and the millennial generation (Strauss and Howe 1991).

In some ways, the millennial generation is a very blessed generation. Their grandparents were labor union organizers and World War II veterans who fought for freedom and equality overseas and at home. These veterans returned home from the war and created the child-centered society of the 1950s and 1960s. For Filipino Americans, the bachelor Manongs married young Filipinas and became fathers well into middle age. Their children, the parents of the millennial generation, were the first cohort with a sizable proportion of college graduates. The millennial generation's grandparents and parents were able to have secure jobs that paid a living wage with benefits. Many became homeowners, remitted money back to their families in the Philippines, sponsored their relatives who wished to become U.S. workers, residents, and citizens, and spoiled their grandchildren and great-grandchildren. Of particular note is the fact that the millennial generation appeared as the United States was again becoming receptive to children. This was in contrast to the period of their predecessors, Generation X. As social critic Neil Howe mentions in his presentations in the United States, Generation X has the dubious distinction of being "the generation whose parents took a pill not to have them."

On the other hand, the millennial generation may be viewed as not so blessed. Baby showers for silent-generation parents were all-female affairs with friends and relatives in homes. By contrast, my boomer friends and I had baby showers at restaurants with men and women guests, many from the workplace. We took birthing and La Leche classes. There was a group of us who took time off from the work force (as either full- or part-time mothers) to be with our children in their formative years. David and Joseph and many of their peers joined play groups, attended nursery school, and participated in endless birthday parties. The 1980s were the start of some mothers talking to their child in utero, and of some parents strategizing on how to get their five-year-old into a "good college." These patterns appear to continue for Nicholas and his digital generation.

Whereas Generation X may have experienced inattention from their parents, the millennial generation experienced a plethora of attention, including micromanagement. The ante was raised, and parents were expected to have "perfect children." The hopes of equality and an end of disparity raised by *Brown v. Board of Education* and by federal programs such as Head Start gave way to nonfederal enrichment programs for the middle and upper classes. Instead of advocating a "level playing field," which is the goal of equal opportunity, there was a shift by the American public from a desire for basic, common standards for all U.S. children to heightened expectations for various groups of students. For example, basic programs providing preventive health care (such as well-child immunizations and screening for vision via the public health system) and nutritious food (via federal breakfast and school-lunch programs) now competed with the more diverse needs of students and the individualized demands of parents. The latter ranged from "mainstreaming" disabled children into classes with regular elementary students to providing more advanced placement courses for high-school students. While some of the millennial generation had parents who were very involved in their development, growth, and formal education, others did not (Csikszentmihalyi and Schneider 2000).

School Days

In the United States, education is viewed as the way to equal opportunity. Representative democracy and a growing economy require educated and appropriately skilled citizens, residents, and workers who have a common knowledge base and who participate actively in civic culture. The public school system of the nineteenth century was instituted to meet these requirements. After World War II, the GI Bill opened up higher education to middle- and working-class Americans. As shown in chapter 3, the children of the pioneer generation and its veterans, within the civil rights movement and the legal arena, fought to ensure the access of people of color and of all the working class to public higher education. And as I discussed in chapter 4, the post-1965 immigrants have been major beneficiaries of the work of prior generations, particularly as regards the achievements of the civil rights movement.

By the end of the twentieth century, equal opportunity for all Americans again was being questioned, especially for people of color and immigrants. This questioning is occurring while the United States faces the need for infrastructural maintenance of its institutions, including educational ones, and as it anticipates the retirement of the massive baby boom generation, including senior educators, amidst budget and trade deficits. The policy question of how resources are to be most equitably allocated is a salient one that must be reexamined. This will require dialogue between the generations and populations who share the common destiny of all Americans. It is of particular concern to Filipino Americans because of the increasing proportion of children of color in the school-age population who will in turn become the future U.S. work force, while supporting a growing elderly dependent population that is, and will be, disproportionately white.

During the 1990s, kindergarten for the millennial generation began to slowly but surely shift from half-day to full-day, and from play time to reading and math readiness. Children were given homework in the first grade. Computers entered the classroom, and it is now a truism that children with home computers have an advantage over those without. At the same time, there was a surge of children of new immigrants. The parents of these children ranged from postdoctoral fellows to persons illiterate in their native tongue, but all shared the dream of equal educational opportunity for their children via the U.S educational system. In some school systems by third grade, children were being screened for programs for the gifted and talented. In seventh grade, a selected few were invited to take SAT tests at Johns Hopkins University's Center for Talented Youth. Meanwhile, students competed in sports and other extracurricular activities, as well as in academic achievement. They were ranked by merit badges and grade-point averages. Like many of their parents, the millennial generation had long commutes between school, extracurricular activities, and home. Like their parents in this information economy, their time was overscheduled; if something had to give it was "down time" or what their parents as children knew as play time or free time (Elkind 2001).

The social shifts that have occurred with the millennial generation are made clearer in a study by Barbara Schneider and David Stevenson on young people in the 1990s and their ambitions.

> The social world of adolescence in the 1990s is more complex than it was in the 1950s. An indicator of this complexity is the number of choices that adolescents make in their schooling, careers, and entertainment. Schooling is more complex because students can choose to study a wider range of subjects, to earn postsecondary degrees in more fields and at more institutions, and to select among numerous financial aid programs to support their efforts. Career choices are more complicated because there are a greater number of jobs, more new types of jobs, and many jobs without well-established career lines. Adolescents also have many more choices in mass entertainment, including movies, television shows, and music. (Schneider and Stevenson 1999, 31)

Their comparison of family circumstances in the 1950s and 1990s also indicates differences.

In the 1950s, being married was highly desirable, and the proportion of people who never married was low, as was the divorce rate. In the 1990s, marriages are less permanent. Whereas 90 percent of children under eighteen lived with their father and mother in 1960, by 1993 this number had declined to 70 percent. Among some of these two-parent families are blended households with children from previous marriages. It has been estimated that in the next decade, because of the rise in single motherhood and divorce rates, 53 percent of children under eighteen will spend some time in one-parent families. If an adolescent does live in a two-parent family, it is likely that both parents work, most often full time. These adolescents see their worlds changing quickly. In general, however, they assume that they will marry later, have children later, be part of dual-career couples, and change jobs more often than their parents . . .

. . . [With respect to higher education and employment,] today's adolescents are more ambitious than those in previous generations. Most high school students plan to attend college, and many of these aspire to jobs as professionals or managers. (Schneider and Stevenson 1999, 31)

What I thought to be a unique finding of this study was the fluidity of the friendships of young Americans today. As the authors note,

Other than best friends, some teenagers considered all others in the school to be associates or acquaintances. Instead of strong peer relationships among juniors and seniors, we found weak ties within peer groups and with others in the school. The perceived distance and level of informality in these relationships appear to have contributed to a sense of being "disconnected" from others in school. (Schneider and Stevenson 1999, 202)

And with respect to the opposite sex,

Boyfriends and girlfriends typically spent more time together with groups of friends than with each other. It appears that the only traditional forms of dating occur when a person asks someone to the junior or senior prom or when a girls asks a boy to a "turnabout dance." For many adolescents, proms or schools dances may be the only conventional "dates" they have in high school. (Schneider and Stevenson 1999, 206)

In general, for children of college-educated, computer-literate "boomer" parents—immigrant or U.S.-born, white or nonwhite—such schedules and competitions were hectic but doable. For children whose parents were not college educated or computer literate, however, a new inequality was born. With respect to computer literacy, this inequality was labeled "the digital divide." Given rapid technological and demographic changes in a compressed time period, the millennial generation was faced with greater divides between "the haves" and "have-nots." While young Filipino Americans are often associated with the "haves," they may also be found among the "have-nots." In a study made between 1992 and 1997 in thirteen school districts across the United States that examined more than a thousand American teenage students and their career preparations, Csikszentmihalyi and Schneider found that

> For most young Americans, the transition to productive occupations has been postponed many years beyond high school graduation. Apparently, the main decision of the last few years of high school is not which career to pursue but which college to attend. The main task of high school is not to prepare students for jobs but to prepare them for further education. What young people need most to take advantage of the opportunities at this stage is good grades in advanced science and math courses, broad knowledge of the world of work, and high ambitions. It also helps to face the future with curiosity and enthusiasm and to have parents who are challenging . . .
>
>   . . . These are some of the essential tools for negotiating successfully the delayed transition to a productive adulthood. Whereas in the past most jobs required more brawn than brains, the reverse is true now. Perhaps for the first time in human history, this is a generation that will make its living from the manipulation of abstract symbols rather than material energy. And this reversal inevitably implies that higher education will play a larger role in preparing young people for the labor market. (Csikszentmihalyi and Schneider 2000, 210)

This suggests a couple of things in relation to the third and fourth generation of Filipino Americans and the children of post-1965 immigrants. First, members of the millennial generation will further be differentiated by their ability to obtain higher education. Second, this education will be a large factor in their ability to compete for jobs that pay a living wage. Given the presence of enduring family ties through generations and high educational expectations among a sizable proportion of Filipino Americans, their youngsters and young adults can be expected to build upon the successes of prior generations of Filipino Americans. Whether these expectations will become reality remains to be seen.

At Mercy High School, my alma mater, today the student body is multiracial and multicultural. Hispanics and Asian Americans, including Filipino Americans, abound. They are increasing not only their proportion of the student population but also that of the scholars and student leaders. Since 1969, Pilipino Studies at San Francisco State University has continued to nurture and graduate Filipino Americans who go on to graduate school and professional schools. At the University of Maryland, College Park, the alma mater of my millennial-generation sons, descendants of the pioneer generation mingle with the children of the post-1965 immigrants; Filipino Americans are active leaders; and a Filipina American has been student-body president. It is not surprising that some of their parents continue to dote on these young adults. They deliver homemade Filipino comfort foods to their children's dorms and apartments and then cart back their laundry. I thought this happened only in the Philippines. My sons wryly observe that the children for whom such care is taken usually have parents who are both post-1965 immigrants. On the other hand, I also know of the Generation X children of post-1965 immigrants who are expected to work not only to pay their college tuition but also to contribute to family expenses, including helping with their siblings' tuition.

The millennial generation of Filipino Americans includes young people who can identify with the new immigrant students portrayed in films such as the British *Bend It Like Beckham*, a story about the senior-high daughter of Pakistani immigrants caught between two cultures, as well as with the jaded, fourth-generation, not-so-model minorities in *Better Luck Tomorrow*. The main character in this film is Ben, a Filipino-American student in a southern California high school who reflects on the murder of a fellow Asian-American high school student by his peers. In any event, young Filipino Americans of the millennial generation are making their presence known as persons with Filipino heritage and as individuals with multiple identities and group memberships.

I remember the stress and pressure placed on David, Joe, and their high-school classmates to get into college in 1998 and 1999. Many of them all along had been good, even great, students, with various extracurricular activities and the required (if not more) hours of community service for graduation. Rob and I had purposely set limits on the number of after-school projects and programs. We managed to eat a warm dinner as a family around the table five nights out of the week. As children and teenagers, this had been one family tradition my husband and I held close. When I was growing up, however, my mom didn't eat dinner with us four nights of the week because of her late work hours as a beautician. And Rob's dad had a job that required travel across the United States for weeks at a time. In terms of our college applications, Rob and I applied to a couple of schools. I don't recall writing any essays. Neither of us prepared for the SAT. David and Joe applied to several schools, crafting their essays on topics that varied by school. Neither of them prepped for the SAT, but they took it more than once to get a higher score, as their dad had done. The eligibility grade-point averages and SAT scores have become highly competitive. Both of my sons had friends with 3.5 grade-point averages and 1200 SAT scores who were wait-listed at state universities. The angst for students applying to elite, private schools is higher. While Rob and I paid for our children's college applications, our friends and neighbors went even further and took time off to tour prospective campuses all over the United States with their children. Friends would weigh the loans they or their children could take out for undergraduate school. When I was in college, the University of California and state university systems did not charge tuition;

Rob attended a private school in Pennsylvania. He recalled that his dad, the head of a one-earner household, paid his tuition as part of the monthly household expenses.

In April 2005, Dave and Joe's younger cousin Araceli was accepted by several high schools—private, parochial, and public—in San Francisco. The Tamayo-Lucas clan was elated. Celi would follow in the steps of Auntie Roni, her dad Bill, and her older cousins Greg and Allan to Lowell. But this milestone was more than the usual. Applying for high school in 2005 was more difficult than applying for college in 1998 or 1999, and Celi applied to almost a dozen high schools. Test scores, recommendations, essays, and hefty application fees were submitted. It was not unusual for Celi, Bill, and Debbie to submit to interviews and a review of financial assets. They all stayed up late at night and spent weekends lining up the applications and meeting due dates. After all these efforts and their joyful outcome, Bill is delighted not to have to pay a five-digit private high-school tuition. He can use the savings for Celi's college fund. Then he begins to wonder about the high-school application process for seven-year-old Renzi, but decides this is a fruitless task for now. Greg and Cassandra, meanwhile, are still focused on elementary school for their four-year-old Nicholas, who will graduate from kindergarten next year.

Joseph and David are now on their own in the Washington, D.C., metro area and the Pacific Northwest, respectively. At the May 2005 Tamayo Family reunion, as they and their cousin Allan strolled up to the stage to be introduced, their Uncle Bill loudly and clearly stated that they were single young men. They were teased about settling down like Greg. Some Filipino Americans still think that marrying as twenty-year-olds is the best for building a family. My brother and I, and certainly our dad, took a different path. In one sense, David and Joseph, like many of their friends and their cousins, have many more choices and opportunities than prior generations had in terms of education, employment, and their personal lives. On the other hand, too many choices can be a dilemma. In any event, after the reunion, I watched them in the Tamayo-Lee dining room play several games in which Araceli and David, the "Type As," were on one side, and Joe "Cool" teamed up with little brother Renzi and littlest cousin Nicholas on the other. Many times, they all seemed to be the same age. Roni, Debbie, and I just chuckled among ourselves.

The search for identity is timeless, especially for young people, as they transition from the protected world of childhood to responsible adulthood. Unlike prior American generations and current non-U.S. cultures, with their rites of passage that mark the end of childhood and the start of manhood or womanhood, contemporary U.S. society celebrates a youth culture that blurs the stages of maturity and responsibility. To some extent, this blur occurs within Filipino and Filipino-American families—for example, where childhood names such as "Baby," "Sonny," and "Junior" follow individuals well into old age. Among some American families, including Filipino-American ones, adult children, usually males in their twenties and even early thirties, still live at home. Others leave but return to the family home and have become known as the boomerang generation. (While this seems to be a phenomenon given much recent attention in the United States, it is not unusual for children in the Philippines and other nations to live with their parents upon the formal completion of their studies, after entry into the workforce, and even after marriage and parenthood.) On the other hand, there are stories of minor-age children who take on adult responsibilities and act as a supplement to or substitutes for their parents, such as by helping raise their younger siblings or by earning income to support their families. All this suggests a state of flux socially and economically.

A FLUID SOCIAL AND ECONOMIC ORDER

There is so much yet to know about these third- and fourth-generation Americans with specific ancestry in the Philippines and also from other cultures. It is not clear that the third and fourth generations of Filipino Americans, or the children and grandchildren of expatriate Filipinos, primarily identify or will continue to identify themselves by race, ethnicity, or ancestry. As noted by psychologist Maria Root,

> Although the geographical location of home for most Filipino Americans may be in the United States or the Philippines (or both), the ancestral home for those in the second, third, fourth, and later generations may reside in the psyche and soul. This symbolic home is nurtured by family stories and historical accounts that document the tragic, heroic, and ordinary ancestors who make our lives possible. (Root 1997, xii–xiii)

Along with other members of their U.S. cohort, third- and fourth-generation Filipino Americans and the children of the post-1965 immigrants are beneficiaries of federal civil rights statutes and policies, and of a multicultural and technologically connected global village. In this environment, they can utilize their relatively new choice and freedom to adapt to and take on situational, fluid, and multiple identities as individuals or group members. With reproductive choice and freedom from subordinate positions based on ascribed characteristics such as sex, race, and national origin, younger Filipino Americans of both sexes can be individuals far more than their grandparents and parents could. Not only do they have a choice to be members of larger social groups, but they also have the choice to be single or a marital partner, or to remain childless or be a parent. They can choose to go from being identified as members of a group to being individuals with multiple identities in multiple places depending on the situation (Lott 1998). This freedom and responsibility to be an individual exists separate from ascriptive or achieved group identity. At the same time, an individual is afforded the ability to choose or not choose to be a member of many social groups.

The freedom to be an individual regardless of group identity, and the concept of the rights of the minority, even a minority of one, are basic and unique features of the United States that were made inherent in 1776 in the Declaration of Independence and in 1790 in the Constitution. Furthermore, in 2005, being an individual in the United States regardless of race, national origin, or sex is possible not only because of equal opportunity policies, which help make the Constitution serve all Americans, but also because of complex economic and social infrastructures in a diverse society and a global economy.

The freedom to be oneself regardless of group identity was previously the domain of white men. For over two centuries, white males in dominant positions and privileged by their race and sex were the only group recognized as individuals. While by and large they were expected to be upstanding members of the status quo and pillars of the community with a wife and children, by comparison they also had the greatest social, educational, employment, and income opportunities. Now these exclusive privileges have been taken away, breaking up the status quo.

Much speculation, research, and analysis concern what will follow the status quo. There is talk in the popular press and dialogue in academia about the "New Economy" and the "New Social Order." Blue Flame Marketing president Jameel Spencer offered related comments in a recent interview with Ashley Collie. Blue Flame Marketing is part of Bad Boy Worldwide Entertainment Group, which is involved in music, publishing, fashion, and film production. In the new fluid social and economic order, observations and comments by business leaders marketing to young Americans can sometimes be particularly noteworthy because they have the advantage of offering a quicker insight into current trends than that offered by scholarly research and long-term studies. In the course of the interview, Spencer noted that

> The next big thing is going to be cross cultural. You're beginning to see it already in the juxtaposition of cultures . . . It's a reflection of the new America. It's about the power of cable and the Internet and people having a better appreciation for one another's cultures. When I was in college, I'd go into the cafeteria. All the black guys sat back here, the white frat guys over there, the artsy fartsy damn-near weirdo cats here, the Asian or Hispanic kids over there. And that's what it was. Now, it's all mixed, everyone's getting along. It ain't about being the same color; it's about, "We are into the same thing." (Collie 2004, 45)

On the face of the New America, he goes on to say,

You can't even tell what his or her racial makeup is. It's like the KKK's worst nightmare, you know what I'm saying, this racial-mixing thing. You could be looking at a light-skinned cat who's Chinese-Jamaican; and you can't tell what he is except he's got a good heart and cares. You walk down the street now in New York, you can't tell where people are from. That's the new America. (Collie 2004, 45)

While his remarks appear to be directed to black adolescents and young men, particularly in the inner city, it is also a message to young people of color, the majority of whom live in urban and suburban areas. This includes young Filipino Americans who may not be upwardly mobile for all sorts of reasons. Spencer says,

I'm the product of a single-parent household. And even though my most impactful vision growing up is of a strong black woman, most will tell you that you can't be successful coming from that background. The revolutionary spirit of hip-hop and this economy that it's spawned is that it's creating individuals like me. It's that type of energy we want to show people. That anything can happen.

What I'd like people to understand most about Blue Flame beyond the marketing and sales stuff, is that we're creating an example of young urban people to see what can happen in life. You may not be able to be Michael Jordan (your jump may never cut it) or Tiger (your golf swing will never be that good), but you can be someone like Jameel Spencer, an upwardly mobile person. So to be a black man who's married with kids and successful in this new urban economy, the most important thing I want to be able to show people is to be tolerant and understanding. (Collie 2004, 45)

Like the generations before them who faced the tensions of Manifest Destiny and common destiny, the millennial and digital generations will lift their voices and offer their contributions to twenty-first-century America. In the winter of 2002–2003, for example, high school students organized and led teach-ins on nonviolence and held class discussions on the merits of a U.S. preemptive war on Iraq. They joined their elders of various religious backgrounds and generations at local and national demonstrations for nonviolence and peace. This was reminiscent of the civil rights movement and earlier peace movements in the 1950s, 1960s, and 1970s. In College Park, my husband and I joined other parents, our son Joseph, and his friends at a 2004 University of Maryland production of the *Vagina Monologues*. The students' enthusiastic performance and audience response reminded me of the then radical 1960s production of *Hair* in my teen-age years. Young men and women of all colors, cultures, and races produced, directed, and enacted the play, with all the proceeds going to various nonprofit programs to help women, including health-care programs and a local shelter for victims of domestic violence. This was consistent not only with their own family and

spiritual values, but it helped them meet a high-school graduation require-
ment of community service.

The millennial generation, along with Generation X, thus far are showing resilience and adaptability in a fluid social and economic order. With the collapse
of the Silicon Valley bubble, a U.S. war in the Middle East, and rising terrorism globally, they understand that they will be the adult leaders in a new America along with the emerging digital generation. This is consistent with the role
of their grandparents and parents, who grew up during the cold war and under
the threat of nuclear war. The beloved grandchildren and great-grandchildren of
the pioneer generation of Filipino Americans will be part of that leadership.

Fortunately, these new Filipino-American leaders can draw from the lessons of the prior generations. In summarizing the lessons from the Filipino
American Young Turks (FAYTS) leadership, Pete Jamero poses and then provides answers to the question of these lessons:

> What can Filipino American communities learn from the FAYTS experience in
> terms of greater participation in the American sociopolitical mainstream? I sug-
> gest three fundamental lessons:
>
> Coalition building and individual participation with mainstream and other mi-
> nority groups must be actively pursued. FAYTS credibility, networking capac-
> ity, and political clout had their roots in FAYTS long-standing working rela-
> tionship with the diversity that is America.
>
> If greater participation in the sociopolitical mainstream is to be accomplished,
> it logically follows that the primary focus and energies of the community must
> be directed to deal with Filipino issues of America, and secondarily to the issues
> of the ancestral "homeland."
>
> Language, regional, and generational differences among Filipinos must be
> bridged. FAYTS was able to bridge these gaps through the ability of key play-
> ers to "fit in" and relate with older or younger Filipinos, Filipinos of mixed eth-
> nicity, and those born and/or raised in the Philippines, regardless of regional af-
> filiation or language facility. (Jamero 1997, 314)

Will these new leaders of the United States be a cohesive civic group? Will they
maintain ties of kinship and hold extended family reunions with attendees from
across coasts and continents? Will they continue to build upon peer relations
honed in the American educational system and marketplace? Will they balance
competitive activities with the collaborative ones that they learned in their me-
diation and conflict-resolution classes in school? Will they strive for individual
improvement over team improvement? What are the human connections in the
postindustrial world that they will reaffirm and create? Will they follow the
shift of Japan and the Western European nations from community and family to
individuality as measured by negative fertility rates? Or will they follow traditional Asian and Hispanic models of family and extended-family orientations?
Will they maintain a commitment to long-term and extended relations?

I have no data, no trends, but I believe our children are our future. For me, as for many Filipinos and Filipino Americans, children are such a joy and treasure. As a mother, for me bringing forth new life and then letting it go is a leap of faith and a vote for the future. For grandmas and great-grandmas, I can only empathize with my sister and mom. In early 1999, I was tapped to be a judge for the annual National History Day program. National History Day is a series of contests on the local, state, and national levels. The approximately two thousand finalists, from the sixth through the twelfth grades and representing all fifty states, spend all day at the University of Maryland, College Park, in spring when the cherry blossoms are in bloom. Their teachers, families, and friends accompany them as they present the findings of their extensive research on topics related to an annual theme. In 1990 the theme was "Rights and Responsibilities in History," and in 2005 it was "Communication in History: The Key to Understanding." These young people present historical papers, exhibits, documentaries, or performances of their own creation. I remember one year when some middle-school students discussed the constitutionality of the internment of Japanese Americans during World War II, and they mentioned the case of Gordon Hirabayashi. I had met Professor Hirabayashi when and I was in college. He was introduced then as the older brother of my professor, Jim Hirabayashi.

Gordon Hirabayashi was a senior at the University of Washington, Seattle, when the Seattle area community of Japanese Americans was ordered to obey curfew limits only for Japanese Americans and to board a bus for internment camps hundreds of miles from Seattle. He refused on the basis that he was U.S.-born citizen and that his constitutional rights should be upheld. His was the first challenge to the government's wartime curfew and expulsion of Japanese Americans, as provided by Executive Order 9066. He was capably represented by the American Civil Liberties Union before the Supreme Court (*Hirabayashi v. the United States*, 1943). The Court, nonetheless, ruled against him 9–0 based on the reasoning that the exclusion, including the curfews and internment, were necessary for national security. Gordon served his prison sentence and afterward continued his college education, becoming one of a handful of Asian Americans at that time to earn a PhD. In the 1970s, younger Asian Americans in search of their history and identity examined more closely the internment period. Other researchers and interested citizens joined them. In 1984 Peter Irons, a political scientist at the University of California, San Diego, uncovered government documents that stated there was no military reason for the exclusion. These materials had been withheld from the Supreme Court. The Hirabayashi case was retried, and in 1987 Gordon's conviction was overturned. On National History Day, based on their independent research, the middle schoolers concluded that Professor Hirabayashi had been vindicated and that the Constitution had been upheld.

In 2004, I was heartened to see more children of color at National History Day, especially in the documentary competition, which I've now been judging since 1999. The theme that year was "Exploration, Encounter and Exchange." A few days after the contest, I was at the National Museum of American History. I was seated at a table at what used to be a nineteenth-century ice-cream parlor now turned into a gelato vendor when I saw some of the contestants. We smiled in recognition of each other. They engaged in rapid conversation with the adults at their table, finished their gelatos, and then shyly came up to me and reintroduced themselves. They wanted to know if I would meet their parents. They were Filipino Americans from central California. The children had told their immigrant parents that in one of the rounds of the competition, they had encountered a Filipino-American judge. Their parents initially thought they might have been mistaken. I was delighted to meet their parents. We were all glad to connect.

I think of all these connections—our generational connections—as I watch Nicholas with his Great-Grandma Anicia pick plums from his Grandpa Fante's garden of California oranges, Filipino vegetables, American Beauty roses, and San Mateo orchids. As his Grandma Roni waters the plants, Nicholas's dad, Gregory, lifts him to reach the higher branches of the plum trees.

WHAT LIES AHEAD

The children and grandchildren of the pioneer generation and the children of the post-1965 immigrants are growing up and thriving overall. They are beloved children of their great-grandparents, grandparents, and parents who previously met the challenges of equality and freedom with the vigilance and action that were needed. Generation X, the millennial generation, and the digital generation are children of the electronic age and of a knowledge economy in a global village. They are growing up in a less-affluent United States, in married and nonmarried family households, and their country faces major budget and trade deficits while fighting a war abroad. Their school, social, and work interactions and experiences are more multicultural and multiracial then those of prior generations. They also have tremendous individual freedom and access to volumes of information. They will be the major players in the next stage toward forging a common destiny.

NOTES

1. The humble but popular Ilocano vegetable stew.
2. Whole roast pig known for its crunchy, crispy fat, and succulent meat.

Chapter Six

The Common Destiny of Multigenerational Americans

> All things are connected. We did not weave the web of life. We are but a strand in it. Whatever befalls the earth befalls the people of earth.
>
> —Chief Seattle on the web of life, 1854

There have been at least four generations of Filipino Americans. They emerged as a direct result of U.S. colonialism in the Philippines in 1898. The first generation, the pioneer generation, came to the United States not as immigrants but as U.S. nationals beginning in the early 1900s. That is a basic but not always obvious point, as Filipino Americans are oftentimes viewed as new immigrants and new Americans, even by post-1965 immigrants. This popular, though not historically accurate, view, can be found in daily news accounts in 2005 of the growing proportions of new immigrants in U.S. neighborhoods, schools, and work places. On a more personal level, I realize that while there are at least four generations of Tamayos, for my sons, Joseph and David, there are at least nine generations of Lotts in the United States—a point poignantly made clear to my children on our annual Memorial Day trips to plant marigolds by their great-grandparent Lotts' headstones in Troutville, Pennsylvania.

At the May 2005 Tamayo family reunion, young, old, and middle-aged participants feasted on a whole roast pig and a huge strawberry sponge cake from the best Chinese bakery in San Francisco. We admired how gracefully we had aged and how beautiful our mothers, spouses, sweethearts, children, and grandchildren were. We scrutinized individual family trees and laughed at old family photos of the Rumbaoas, Thamys, and Tamayo progeny. As we took our individual multigenerational family portraits and then posed for the grand clan photo, we realized that we are a family and a community composed of both longtime residents and newcomers. Many of us are multiracial Filipinos with various ancestries. Many of us are also multilingual. I think there are several important strengths or values that Filipino Americans can offer future generations of the United States. First, a comfort with and long-time experience in being open, inclusive, caring, and adaptable by language, culture, and race—traits that help Filipino Americans ensure smooth interpersonal relations and maintain connections. A Filipino adage says that it is better to bend like the bamboo than break like the oak, a philosophy that ensures the adaptability future generations.

Second, the unique legacy of Filipino Americans as U.S. nationals distinguishes them as a truly American people. Their democratic heritage is clearly based on the U.S. model. The residents of the Philippines revolted against Spanish colonization for the right to self-rule just as the American revolutionaries revolted against the British monarchy. As U.S. nationals, Filipinos of my parents' generation were educated and nurtured as children under the U.S. public school and public heath systems. Healthy and educated children are a prerequisite to a stable democracy. As for the relatives and friends of my parents who decided that their future was in the Philippines, they continued the call for self-determination as they worked in peaceful cooperation with the United States to transform the Philippines from a U.S. colony into the Republic of the Philippines. In 1986, current and potential democracies around the world were inspired by the courage and peacefulness of the Filipino people who abolished the corrupt government of Ferdinand Marcos in the People Power Revolution. Filipinos, both laity and clergy, revolted against a corrupt presidential election. The Filipino religious were visible leaders in the outcry against the Marcos government and in the demand for a restoration of democracy and social justice. A powerful image of that era remains that of seminarians and nuns with rosaries and young girls with flowers persuading Filipino soldiers to lay their arms down. This was a moment of pride shared by Filipino Americans. The confluence of the laity and the religious showed that in addition to democratic principles, the Filipino people are sustained by their spiritual strength, including the Catholicism of their Spanish heritage. This is consistent with other nonviolence movements enacted by citizens who wanted to exercise their fundamental rights by embracing spiritual and moral dimensions. In modern history, the most notable of these were the Indian nationalist movement led by Mahatma Gandhi in the 1940s against British colonialism and the U.S. civil rights movement in the 1950s and 1960s led by the Reverend Dr. Martin Luther King Jr.

Third, Filipino Americans have a massive civic-democratic heritage in the United States. Unfortunately, this has not been well documented for several reasons. An obvious reason is the fact that Filipino Americans first came to the United States as a community of single young men, primarily manual laborers, who were never meant to be permanent residents. Another is that for a long time Filipino Americans were a very small population, even including women and children. Initially, they settled on the West Coast and in Hawaii and Chicago and, like other Asian Americans, were not visible to the rest of the nation. A not-so-obvious reason is that the silent and baby boom generations—which would include my siblings and me—were raised to be Americans with Filipino ancestry. Our parents expected us to be perfect in our written and oral English. The memories of Spanish colonizers who had seized their ancestors' lands because the latter could not read, write, or speak Spanish were fresh in our parents' minds. In addition, my dad and his generation believed that a person of culture and a cosmopolitan view should be literate in many languages. Our allegiance in terms of civic participation—voting, serving in the military, taking advantage of our access to higher education in the United States—is a common story of children of immigrants who are establishing roots in a new home. The nisei generation, the first U.S.-born generation of Japanese immigrants, are a good example of children raised to be the model minority or, in the words of some social scientists, "to outwhite the whites." Even as the Japanese Americans were interned during World War II as a military threat, Japanese-American Boy Scout Troop 343 and six other scout troops at Heart Mountain Camp in Wyoming earned merit badges and advanced in rank. They persevered even as attempts by scout leaders to invite fellow scouts from the neighboring communities of Powell and Cody, Wyoming, initially met with resistance (Aratani 2005). In 2005 by contrast, Generation X, the millennial generation, and the digital generation of Asian Americans have the freedom to see themselves as group members or as individuals beyond race and ethnicity.

Another unapparent reason for the lack of documentation of Filipino Americans' civic heritage is that in the post–World War II era, the Filipino nation and Filipino nationals were just developing. Thus, while the Filipino generations born and reared in the United States knew of regional and family history through organizations such as the Laoaguenos and Pampangans, we saw our parents' civic participation as personal history and not as something necessarily to be shared or documented for posterity. It was only with our evolving recognition that the United States is greater than a black-white society, the establishment of ethnic studies programs in the late 1960s, and with the perseverance of the Filipino American National Historical Society that painstaking scholarship began to uncover this rich heritage. This heritage includes the leadership of union organizing since the first generation began working on Hawaii plantations in the early 1900s. In recent decades, Filipino Americans' best-known demonstration of union organizing was the founding of the United Farm Workers Union with Cesar Chavez in the 1960s. Less well known is the strong union membership among the pioneer generation that provided that generation with a living wage and benefits, which in turn allowed them to enter the American middle class and to raise the second generation with a social safety net.

Through times of peace and war, Filipino Americans have served and continue to serve in the armed forces with distinction. The valor of World War II Filipino-American soldiers is now recognized by both the Filipino-American community and the U.S. government, and has been described in documentaries such as Sonny Izon's *An Untold Triumph*, and in U.S. research as reflected in Alex Fabros's *In Honor of Our Fathers: The Boogie-Woogie Boys: A History of Filipino Americans in World War II*. It goes without saying that Filipino Americans are well represented in the U.S. military service, even at the rank of Army general, specifically, by Major General Antonio Taguba and Lieutenant General Edward Soriano. The U.S. Navy has long recruited Filipinos. Navy Rear Admiral Dr. Connie Mariano served as president's physician in President Clinton's administration. Dr. Mariano was the first Filipino American to reach the rank of admiral. Her father, Angel Mariano, entered the U.S. Navy as a steward, served under six admirals, and rose to the rank of Master Chef (Marquez 2000, 42–45). In addition, Filipino Americans have proven their ability to serve the U.S. government and the interests of American working men and women. In terms of electoral participation, since the 1970s Filipino Americans have run for and sometimes won elected office, especially at the local level as mayors, city council members, and board of education members. Further, David Valderrama of the state of Maryland, Velma Veloria of Washington, and Jon Amores of West Virginia have served in their state legislatures after being elected through a broad, multigenerational, multicultural coalition. Filipinos have long been represented in the state government of Hawaii since Hawaii became the fiftieth state. In 1996, Benjamin Cayetano became the first Filipino governor of Hawaii and the first Filipino governor in U.S. history. In Hawaii, Filipino Americans have also made their entry into the judicial branch of government. In April 1974, Benjamin Menor became the first Filipino American to sit on the Hawaii Supreme Court. In May 2000, Filipino Associate Justice Simeon Acoba and Associate Justice Mario Ramil were two of the five justices of the Supreme Court of the State of Hawaii (Tamoria 2000, 20–22).

Filipino Americans across the generations continue to use their legacy and skills of social participation as manifest in their formidable presence in the health-care, hospitality, and dependent-care (from child care to elder care to disability care) industries. While there is much anecdotal evidence, we have yet to document the contributions and influence of pioneer generation member Corazon Llacuna and other unsung heroines like her. My Auntie Cora graduated from the University of the Philippines with a nursing degree. After World War II, she and her husband, Frank Llacuna, one of the first Filipino-American pharmacists, settled in Los Angeles. Auntie Cora worked her way up from staff to management positions at Queen of Angels Hospital and brought along a host of other Filipino-American health-care personnel with her. In the 1950s and 1960s our families would visit one another. The Llacunas came to San Francisco more often than the Tamayos went to Los Angeles. When they visited us, they would bring along young Filipino student nurses to see the Bay Area and to meet relatives. When my family visited Uncle Frank, Auntie Cora, and Eleanor and Shirley, their home was a focal point for young medical students and other hospital employees who constantly came in and out looking for a home-cooked Filipino meal, advice on how to prepare for an interview or how to act on a date, or just to hang out.

The third and fourth Filipino-American generations, along with the children and grandchildren of the post-1965 immigrants, have a multicultural, multiracial, and multilingual heritage, high-tech skills, and the interpersonal and intergenerational communication skills that allow them to work and play across all populations, both native and foreign born, for a productive destiny in common with all Americans. In a way, this last point suggests not a final chapter but a new beginning, not a historical point of view but a futurist one beyond ethnicity and race. As I noted in the preface to this book, the historical social order of inequality has been primarily in terms of color. The present divide is much more complex, with nuances and implications that will affect the survival of this nation.

For the third, fourth, and subsequent generations of Filipino Americans, their legacy will be based on their ability to transform themselves from children, followers, and dependents to adults, leaders, and citizens of the United States of America. At the same time, they will also be emerging as world citizens faced with ensuring future generations a common destiny. The unfolding story of 2005 is a multigenerational one of common connections. My contribution to this unfolding narrative is limited to three scenarios that other storytellers and researchers will enrich. These are the scenario of growing old in America, of balancing individual rights and common interests, and of living out a common destiny in today's global village.

GROWING OLD IN AMERICA

One of the poignancies of the belated efforts being made to tell the story of Filipino and Filipino-American soldiers and to obtain their due benefits as war veterans is that those veterans are passing on into history. My father and many of my uncles have already died. One of the reasons I have written this book is that my mother and aunts are now at the last stage of life. Despite the urging of Fred and Dorothy Cordova, founders of the Filipino American National Historical Society, who since the 1980s have encouraged oral interviews of the members of the pioneer generation, the stories of the Man-angs are even less known than the stories of the Manongs. The personal stories and collective history of the pioneer generation need to be told not just for their great-grandchildren but for all American children so that they can fulfill their own destinies in U.S. democracy.

In the Philippines, as in many Asian, Latino, Indian, African, and other cultures that predate U.S. culture, the elderly are treated with great respect and love. They are the wise men and women of the village. Among Filipino Americans, they are addressed as *Lola* (Grandmother), or *Lolo* (Grandfather), or *Apo*, which means "god" in Ilocano. Because my father and uncles married women who were much younger than they were, these couples understood that the Manangs would most likely outlast the Manongs. They understood the need for providing for their families and recognized the possibility that their children might grow up fatherless. Fortunately, they were able to form families and raise children when reciprocal rights and responsibilities between the federal government and U.S. citizens and residents, and between employers and employees, as represented in the Social Security Act of 1935, were foremost. In the final years of the Manongs, many of their wives nursed them at home, often with aid from family and friends, sometimes while they were still in the paid labor force, and always with great faith. While some Filipino-American families are multigenerational, with grandparents, children, and grandchildren living under the same roof, many are not. Like other Americans of the "sandwich generation," Filipino-American adult children are faced with moving their parents from their homes to alternative housing, such as assisted-living centers, even as they are caring for their own children still at home. They are also using their professional and business skills in the health-care and hospitality industries to establish a range of dependent-care facilities, from group homes to nursing homes for the elderly and other dependent adults.

Filipina domestic workers, along with other immigrant women from Africa, Latin America, and Asia, increasingly are providing care for dependent Americans at both ends of the life cycle. This is an example of a historical shift in the division of labor. Filipina domestic workers have replaced black women in the North and South[1] and, to a lesser extent, Latina women in the Southwest in this type of work. My mom has spoken of the kindness of the Filipino male caregivers in her assisted-living residence who treat her as their grand aunt. When she or my aunts and uncles are hospitalized for various age-related illnesses, they are oftentimes tended by Filipino and Filipino-American technicians, nurses, and doctors.

The aging of the U.S. population stems from increasing human longevity and decreasing population growth. According to a recent Population Reference Bulletin,

For most of human history, world population never exceeded 10 million people. The death rate was about as high as the birth rate, and the rate of population growth was scarcely above zero. Significant population growth began about 8000 B.C., when humans began to farm and raise animals. By 1650, world population had expanded about 50 times—from 10 million to 5000 million. Then world population shot up another 500 million in just 150 years, reaching its first billion around 1800. It achieved its second billion by 1903, 130 years later; a third billion by 1960, only 30 years later; and a fourth billion by 1975, just 15 years later. But the last fifth and sixth billion (attained in 1987 and 1999), took just over a decade each. Although the pace of world population growth has slowed, we still expect another billion added before 2015. (McFalls 2003, 32)

The sizable growth rates of the U.S. population in the twentieth century were due in large part to the unexpectedly high fertility rates of American women as 10 million men returned home from World War II (Beale 2004). Thus far, they have produced the largest cohort in U.S. history, the baby boomers, although the millennial generation exhibits a comparable size with both the children of native-born and new immigrants. In addition, the U.S. population increased tremendously in the latter half of the twentieth century due to the repeal of the exclusionary Immigration Act of 1924 and the McCarran-Walter Act of 1952, and also as a result of the implementation of more inclusive immigration and refugee policies beginning with the 1965 amendments to the Immigration and Nationality Act. In 2004, the United States is the third most populous nation in the world, after China and India.

How Americans deal with an increasing proportion of the U.S. population that is living longer and with more years of dependent care due to acute and long-term chronic conditions will be the new terrain that challenges the viability of common destiny. That terrain will be primarily along generational lines, but it will also have racial and economic components because whites will be disproportionately older and wealthier, and nonwhites will be disproportionately younger and poorer. The U.S. experience with growing older is also occurring globally as an aging Western Europe and Japan must also weigh negative replacement birth rates with population reproduction and economic production via immigrants from different cultures, religions, and races. Americans increasingly are finding it more difficult to physically escape from the tensions of population density. There are no more frontiers in the United States, and rural areas continue to make way for nonrural ones. With ambivalence and reluctance, Americans are facing the demographic reality of aging and death. This is problematic for a youth-oriented culture. While cultures with strong spiritual and extended family ties, including the culture of Filipino Americans, are able to cope with the different stages of the life cycle, which include death as a part of the natural order, Americans over the generations have become more secular and individual-oriented. In 2005, new

American immigrants, including Filipinos, bring with them worldviews that acknowledge human mortality as part of the web of life.

BALANCING INDIVIDUAL RIGHTS
AND COMMON INTERESTS

America's founding settlers envisioned and established a government of the people, by the people, and for the people via elected representatives. In addition, as strong and independent personalities, they also recognized the importance of the individual. Over time, this recognition of both group and individual rights and of minority and majority rights, has become the unique legacy of the United States. The freedom of and responsibility in being an individual exists separate from ascriptive or achieved group identity. At the same time, an individual is afforded the mobility to choose or not choose to be a member of many social groups (Lott 1998). This liberty of persons to be both individuals and members of various social groups inspires the immigration to America from all over the world of similar persons who seek the freedom to be whoever they want to be. The interplay between individual and collective identity is played out generally among young persons testing or rebelling against adults. In the United States, the post–World War II decades saw the emergence of a distinct youth population—teenagers—that could be viewed separately from their identity as members of a family and therefore under adult supervision. Among immigrant populations, this assertion of individual rather than collective identity is played out in the question "Who am I?" For generations of Filipino Americans, the more specific question is "Am I Filipino? Am I Filipino American? Or am I American?"

As for the pioneer generation of my dad and my uncles, they made the distinction that their ancestry was Filipino but their citizenship was American. Also, they were young men in search of new lives and were not content with settling for old ways. Certainly their hearts belonged to both the Philippines and the United States. But they decided to raise their families where they envisioned a fresh start and a promising future. The United States was created in the New World. It was a place to start anew. An individual left the Old World with its old traditions and connections. In America, one could remake oneself and not be group member. One could change a family name that denoted ancestry in the Old World and opt for a surname that was less ethnic oriented, a surname such as "Smith" or "Baker." In the Tamayo family, my cousin Pedro Tamayo changed his name to Peter Thamy when he enlisted in the armed forces. This was not unusual among first- and second-generation Americans. The change was in part for the sake of having an easier-topronounce, more "American sounding" name. At the same time, with such a change the link to the Tamayo name, for example, for succeeding generations was altered. The point is that in America, one can be an individual separate from any group, even to the point of severing one's intergenerational connections. An individual can have a different persona and can even re-create himself or herself over time. This option is not limited to entertainers or other celebrities but is available to regular people as the shifting of sexual identity, family identity, and racial identity have become more visible to and more commonly recognized by (though sometimes reluctantly) the public. Sexual orientation may be changed over time, and individuals may even, through modern technology, change their gender. Clan and basic group identities, previously expressed primarily through the pater familias role of the male, and through wives assuming their husband's surname and children assuming their father's surname, have been challenged in this age of individual freedom. Feminists under the leadership of Gloria Steinem and *Ms.* magazine offered the honorific *Ms.* to denote women as individuals, separate from their marital status as clearly ascribed in the honorifics of *Mrs.* and *Miss.* Similarly, the academic and public discourse in the 1990s concerning individuals and organized groups that did not want to be classified as one race only but as multiracial or of no race was another shift from group identity to individual identity. These experiences have shown us that individuals can choose to be members of different groups, or not, and can assume different identities in different situations, usually for their personal advantage. These changes occurred during the agricultural and industrial eras in U.S. development. The information age, with its virtual reality, including anonymity and multiple identities, will extend individuality to another stage.

Much of U.S. history and indeed, most of human history, has been devoted to ensuring economic and physical survival of the group. The elaborate infrastructural systems of defense and social security programs established after the Depression and World War II may be viewed as the hallmark of an intergenerational responsibility for mutual survival. With the postwar affluence, creation of a welfare state and a leisure class seemed to be a next logical step in life, liberty, and the pursuit of happiness. Writing about the growth of the creative class in the information age, Richard Florida states, "The rise of an affluent or 'post-scarcity' economy means that we no longer have to devote all our energies just to staying alive, but have the wealth, time and ability to enjoy other aspects of life. This in turn affords us choices we did not have before" (Florida 2002, 81). Florida goes on to quote Ronald Inglehart:

An intergenerational shift from emphasis on economic and physical security toward increasing emphasis on self-expression, subjective well-being, and quality of life . . . This cultural shift is found throughout advanced industrial societies;

it seems to emerge among birth cohorts that have grown up under conditions in
which survival is taken for granted. (Florida 2002, 82)

In the information age, Americans seem to be moving away from the Protestant Ethic that defined an individual's relation and responsibility to the divine;
and just as important, from the social contract of mutual rights and responsibilities laid out in the Constitution and reaffirmed in the Gettysburg Address
of President Abraham Lincoln, the "Four Freedoms" set forth in President
Franklin Roosevelt's 1941 State of the Union address, and the 1963 speech "I
have a dream" by the Reverend Dr. Martin Luther King Jr. Are Americans
moving toward autonomy and individuality without the firm connections of
reciprocity and the ties inherent in their common destiny and in the motto
E pluribus unum? Or, as Robert Putnam observed, "Are we bowling alone?"
(2000). Or again, as Richard Florida subsequently declared, "We acknowledge that there is no corporation or other large institution that will take care
of us—that we are truly on our own" (2002, 115).

And yet, despite the rise of single-person households in the United States
and the explosion of products targeting the individual—such as one-serving
meals or such self-centered messages as "You're worth it"—the connections
between groups and across generations continue. For centuries and in all cultures the human connection has spoken of shared responsibility, group accountability, and a collective conscience. In the United States we are
painfully watching this timeless fact of life play out as the bishops of the
Catholic Church deal with child abuse by the clergy; as employees, share-
holders, and the American public deal with corporate leaders who put themselves before the public interest; and as American and other soldiers again
pay the ultimate sacrifice for a war of choice, a war of Manifest Destiny.

The American experiment is in the middle of its first test of the twenty-first
century. Can the Americans who have achieved new heights of individualism
come together again to be patriots and citizen soldiers? Can they reaffirm the
generational connections that have been safeguarded by the Declaration of Independence, the Constitution, the Bill of Rights; by public institutions such
as the executive, legislative, and judicial branches of government; by families
and community or civic organizations; by public schools and universities, a
public health service, and a public safety net? Can Americans balance individual rights with generational responsibilities, and in so doing honor those
who came before them and nurture those who come after them? The above
questions are not academic. My sons pose the question, "Mom, who do you
think is going to choose your nursing home?" with a smile, but it is indeed
their generation and that of Nicholas who will creatively find the answers to
these questions.

cence of a consumption-based economy, or will the U.S. rise again out of the ashes like the fabled phoenix and soar like the American national symbol, the bald eagle? In the twenty-first century, a diverse lot of U.S. citizens and residents forms a new mainstream, which is taking its turn at reshaping U.S. destiny. Future world historians will look back at these citizens and residents of the United States in 2005 to see whether we acted wisely on the behalf of the generations that will follow Nicholas and his generation.

NOTES

1. After the civil rights movement, black women moved out of domestic work and into professional, administrative, and technical positions.

COMMON DESTINY IN THE GLOBAL VILLAGE

There is no longer an Old World or even a New World. There is only a global village. Prosperity and peace, as well as poverty and war transcend national borders. As the Reverend Dr. Martin Luther King Jr. prophetically stated before his 1968 assassination, the choice facing us is not between violence and nonviolence but between nonviolence and nonexistence. As noted in the epigraph to this chapter, Chief Seattle foresaw the same destiny in 1854, for truly, "whatever befalls the earth befalls the people of earth."

The opportunities of American freedom stemming from diffusion of knowledge and the enforcement of equal opportunities resonate deeply among peoples around the world, making the United States a magnet that continues to attract immigrants. The United States draws intellectual and social capital from all regions of the world, including the developing world, with its younger, vibrant, and hopeful populations. More and more, the United States is a microcosm of the world in its culture, ancestry, creed, and language. Its citizens have origins and roots from all over the world, and so the United States is connected by these ties of kinship to all nations. This can be a critical asset for this nation because at this point in human history, the United States is the only superpower on the globe. Also at this time, great divisions exist among the American people regarding the future direction of this nation, and other nation-states question this U.S. global leadership.

In order to meet the challenges of internal and external dissension and of threatening epidemics and wars—which do not necessarily respect national boundaries—the United States will need to draw from its multicultural population and as well from the populations of its fellow nations. War and disease are beyond human command and beyond the control of reason and technology. Mutual survival is still dependent on deep, nonrational human connections such as instinct, trust in one another, and faith in the divine. Filipino Americans, whether the descendants of the pioneer generation or the post-1965 immigrants, place a high priority on formal education and technology, yet they cling to their rosaries and daily devotions. Not only the elderly widows and widowers of my mother's generation but also the younger, highly educated Filipino professionals of later generations gather routinely in various religious organizations, traditional and evangelical.

Throughout human history, mankind has fallen from grace only to rise again. The biblical battles of Michael and Lucifer, Cain and Abel, and David and Goliath continue in the information age. Even as science, technology, and reason became the powers that defined the industrial and information ages, these newer gods continued to exist side-by-side with the power of faith, which from time immemorial has been directed to that realm that is beyond

Epilogue

It is Memorial Day weekend. This holiday which honors America's fallen soldiers since the Civil War, was once known as Decoration Day. I didn't know that until 1985 when Rob, David, Joseph, their Grandma Eleanor, and I first accompanied Rob's Aunt Deedee and Uncle Kermit to decorate the Lott Family Cemetery in Troutville, Pennsylvania. The annual Memorial Day weekend trip became a family tradition. The cemetery is behind Trinity United Church of Christ. Next to the church is Rob's Great-Grandpa Frederick Lott's Victorian home with its huge front porch and a widow's walk on the roof. Troutville is one of those small, one-street towns in the Pennsylvania mountains. We would reach it after a six-hour drive, with the last thirty miles filled with newly plowed fields, deep-purple mountain laurels, and orange-blossomed azaleas. As we wound our way around the back roads, David and Joseph would keep a tally of the groundhog roadkill and the Amish buggies. At the cemetery, they would help their dad carry buckets of water to their Great-Grandpa and Grandpa Josephs' graves and watch Uncle Kermit plant multi-colored and yellow marigolds. They'd run around looking at the various headstones, figuring out which was the oldest, who died as an infant, and who was the child of whom. They always got a kick out of seeing their names on the headstones. Robert Lott was nineteen years old, a serviceman in the ball turret of a U.S. Air Force Flying Fortress when he died in 1945 overseas. There are at least two Joseph Henry Lotts.

In 2005, it is just Rob and I, and we are planting flowers on his mother's grave for the first time since her death last fall. David is competing in an ultimate Frisbee tournament in Carlsbad, Oregon. Joseph is playing on the beach at Ocean City, Maryland, a long-standing Memorial Day tradition for younger generations. Their cousin Gregory is marching down the aisle to receive his MBA in San Jose, California. His son, Nicholas, is waiting anxiously for his new sibling due July 4. His mom and dad, Roni and Fante, are boarding a Japanese Airlines flight to Manila and from there will go on to attend the wedding of Fante's niece in Cabadbaran, Agusan del Norte, Mindanao, Philippines.

I am looking at the photos from the May 7 First Tamayo Family Reunion and thinking how fortunate we all are to have one another. I am anxious to send the best photos to my mom, especially the one with her grandchildren and great-grandchild. I also make a mental note to write a long thank-you letter to my cousin, Norma.

References

Alcantara, Ruben R. 1981. *Sakada: Filipino Adaptation in Hawaii*. Washington, D.C.: University Press of America.

Alegado, Dean. 2002. "Filipino Americans in the U.S. Labor Movement." Panel presentation, National Museum of American History, Smithsonian Institution, December 11.

Aluit, Alfonso J. 1968. *Philippines*. Singapore: Felta Books Sales.

Aratani, Lori. 2005. "Painful Times, Pleasant Memories." *Washington Post*, July 12, A3.

Bacho, Peter. 1997. "The Tragic Sense of Filipino History." In Root, *Filipino American: Transformation and Identity*.

Barlow, William, and Peter Shapiro. 1971. *An End to Silence: The San Francisco State Student Movement in the 60s*. New York: Pegasus.

Beale, Calvin. 2004. "Reflections on 50+ Years as a Federal Demographic Statistician." *AMSTATNews* 322 (April): 6–8.

Bloch, Louis. 1930. *Facts about Filipino Immigration into California*. Special bulletin no. 3. State of California, Department of Industrial Relations. Reprint, R and E Research Associates: San Francisco, 1972.

Bonacich, Edna. 1984. "United States Capital Development: A Background to Asian Immigration." In *Labor Immigration under Capitalism: Asian Workers in the United States before World War II*, ed. Lucie Cheng and Edna Bonacich. Berkeley: University of California Press.

Boyle, Kay. 1970. *The Long Walk at San Francisco State*. New York: Grove.

Brown, Claude. 1965. *Manchild in the Promised Land*. New York: Macmillan.

Brubaker, William Rogers. 1989. *Immigration and the Politics of Citizenship in Europe and North America*. Lanham, Md.: University Press of America.

Bulosan, Carlos. 1946. *America Is in the Heart: A Personal History*. New York: Harcourt, Brace.

Cariño, Benjamin V. 1987. "The Philippines and Southeast Asia: Historical Roots and Contemporary Linkages." In Fawcett and Carino, *Pacific Bridges*.

Cheng, Lucie, and Edna Bonacich, eds. 1984. *Labor Immigration under Capitalism: Asian Workers in the United States before World War II*. Berkeley: University of California Press.

Choy, Catherine Ceniza. 2003. *Empire of Care: Nursing and Migration in Filipino American History*. Durham, N.C.: Duke University Press.

Chua, Amy. 2003. *World on Fire: How Exporting Free Market Democracy Breeds Ethnic Hatred and Global Instability* New York: Doubleday.

Collie, Ashley Jude. 2004. "Getting Hip to the New American Economy." *Southwest Airlines Spirit*, March.

Cordova, Fred. 1983. *Filipinos, Forgotten Asian Americans: A Pictorial Essay, 1763–circa 1963*. Dubuque, Iowa: Kendall/Hunt.

Csikszentmihalyi, Mihaly, and Barbara Schneider. 2000. *Becoming Adult: How Teenagers Prepare for the World of Work*. New York: Basic Books.

De la Cruz, Enrique B., and Pearlie Rose S. Baluyut, eds. and curators. 1998. *Confrontations, Crossings, Convergence: Photographs of the Philippines and the United States, 1898–1998*. Los Angeles: University of California Asian American Studies Center and the University of California Southeast Asia Program.

Dimas, Nicasio Jr., Donald Chou, and Phyllis K. Fong. 1980. *The Tarnished Golden Door: Civil Rights Issues in Immigration*. Report of the United States Commission on Civil Rights. Washington, D.C.: U.S. Government Printing Office.

DuBois, W. E. B. 1971. *Dusk of Dawn: An Essay toward an Autobiography of Race Concepts*. New York: Schocken Books.

Elkind, David. 2001. *The Hurried Child: Growing Up Too Fast Too Soon*. Cambridge, Mass.: Perseus.

Espiritu, Yen Le. 2003. *Home Bound: Filipino Americans Living across Cultures, Communities and Countries*. Berkeley: University of California Press.

Evangelista, Susan. 1985. *Carlos Bulosan and His Poetry: A Biography and Anthology*. Quezon City: Ateneo de Manila University Press.

Fabros, Alex S. Jr. 1994. *In Honor of Our Fathers: The Boogie-Woogie Boys: A History of Filipino Americans in World War II*. Presentation at the National Museum of American History, Smithsonian Institution, October 11.

Fawcett, James T., and Benjamin V. Cariño, eds. 1987. *Pacific Bridges: The New Immigration from Asia and the Pacific Islands*. Staten Island, N.Y.: Center for Migration Studies.

———. 1987. "International Migration and Pacific Basin Development," in Fawcett and Cariño, *Pacific Bridges*.

Florida, Richard. 2002. *The Rise of the Creative Class and How It's Transforming Work, Leisure, Community and Everyday Life*. New York: Basic Books.

Foner, Nancy, Ruben Rumbaut, and Stephen J. Gold, eds. 2000. *Immigration Research of a New Century: Multidisciplinary Perspectives*. New York: Russell Sage Foundation.

———. 2000. "Immigration and Immigration Research in the United States." In Foner, Rumbaut, and Gold, *Immigration Research of a New Century*.

Foner, Philip S. 1976. *We, the Other People: Alternative Declarations of Independence by Labor Groups, Farmers, Women's Rights Advocates, Socialists, and Blacks, 1829–1975*. Urbana: University of Illinois Press.

Fong-Torres, Ben. 1994. *Rice Room: Growing Up Chinese-American, from Number Two Son to Rock 'n' Roll*. New York: Hyperion.

Franklin, Benjamin. 1751. "Observations Concerning the Increase of Mankind." Quoted in Roger Daniels, *Coming to America*. New York: HarperCollins, 1990.

Glazer, Nathan, and Daniel Moynihan. 1963. *Beyond the Melting Pot: The Negroes, Puerto Ricans, Jews, Italians, and Irish of New York City*. Cambridge, Mass.: MIT Press.

Guerreo, Rio M. 2003. "Dual Citizenship: To Be or Not to Be?" *Filipinas* 12, no. 138 (October).

Hirabayashi, Lane Ryo, Akemi KikumuraYano, and James A. Hirabayashi, eds. 2002. *New Worlds, New Lives: Globalization and People of Japanese Descent in the Americas and from Latin America in Japan*. Stanford, Calif.: Stanford University Press.

Howe, Neil, and William Strauss. 2000. *Millennials Rising: The Next Great Generation*. London: Vintage.

Hune, Shirley. 1977. *Pacific Migration to the United States: Trends and Themes in Historical and Sociological Literature*. RIEES bibliographic studies no. 2. Washington, D.C.: Research Institute on Immigration and Ethnic Studies, Smithsonian Institution.

Jamero, Peter M. 1997. "The Filipino American Young Turks of Seattle." In Root, *Filipino Americans: Transformation and Identity*.

Janeway, Michael. 2004. *The Fall of the House of Roosevelt: Brokers of Ideas and Power from FDR to LBJ*. New York: Columbia University Press.

Jaynes, Gerald, and Robin Williams Jr., eds. 1989. *A Common Destiny: Blacks and American Society*. Washington, D.C.: National Academy Press.

Jensen, Leif, and Yoshimi Chitose. 1996. "Today's Second Generation: Evidence from the 1990 Census." In Portes, *The Second Generation*.

Kelly, Patricia Fernandez. 1996. "Divided Fates: Immigrant Children and the New Assimilation." In Portes, *The Second Generation*.

Kennedy, John Fitzgerald. 1964. *A Nation of Immigrants*. New York: Harper and Row.

Kingston, Maxine Hong. 1977. *Woman Warrior: Memoirs of a Girlhood among Ghosts*. New York: Alfred A. Knopf.

Kitano, Harry. 1969. *Japanese Americans: The Evolution of a Subculture*, Englewood Cliffs, N.J.: Prentice-Hall.

Kuhn, Thomas. 1962. *The Structure of Scientific Revolutions*. Chicago: University of Chicago Press.

Levy, Frank, and Richard Nurname. 2004. *The New Division of Labor*. Princeton, N.J.: Princeton University Press.

Lott, Juanita Tamayo. 2003. "Love Is What They Give." *Filipinas* 11, no. 119 (March).

———. 1998. *Asian Americans: From Racial Category to Multiple Identities*. Walnut Creek, Calif.: AltaMira.

———. 1997. "The Demographic Changes Transforming the Filipino American Community." In Root, *Filipino Americans: Transformation and Identity*.

———. 1993. "The Changing Significance of Race for People of Color." *Trotter Review* 7, no. 2 (Fall): 4–7.

———. 1989. *Knowledge and Access: A Study of Asian and Pacific American Communities in the Washington, D.C. Metropolitan Area*. Washington, D.C.: Office of the Assistant Secretary for Public Service, Smithsonian Institution.

———. 1980. "Migration of a Mentality: The Pilipino Community." In *Asian-Americans: Social and Psychological Perspectives*, ed. Russell Endo, Stanley Sue, and Nathaniel N. Wagner, vol. 2. Palo Alto, Calif.: Science and Behavior Books.

Lyman, Stanford. 1973. "Japanese-American Generation Gap." *Society* 10, no. 2 (January/February).

Magtalas, Emmily. 2004. "The Care Business." *Filipinas* 13, no. 145 (May).

Maier, Thomas. 2003. *The Kennedys: America's Emerald Kings*. New York: Basic Books.

Marquez, Romeo P. 2000. "In the Line of Fire: Dr. Connie Mariano, the President's Physician." *Filipinas* 9, no. 98 (November).

Martin, Philip, and Elizabeth Midgley. 2003. "Immigration: Shaping and Reshaping America." *Population Bulletin* 58, no. 2 (June).

McFalls, William A. Jr. 2003. "Population: A Lively Introduction." *Population Bulletin* 58, no. 4 (December).

McWilliams, Carey. 1942. *Brothers under the Skin*. Boston: Little, Brown.

Mills, C. Wright. 1959. *The Sociological Imagination*. London: Oxford University Press.

Morales, Royal F. 1974. *Makibaka: The Pilipino Struggle*. Los Angeles: Mountainview.

Moss, David. 2002. *When All Else Fails: Government as the Ultimate Risk Manager*. Cambridge: Harvard University Press.

Myrdal, Gunnar. 1944. *An American Dilemma: The Negro Problem and Modern Democracy*. New York: Harper.

Nakashima, Ellen, and Edward Cody. 2004. "Filipinos Take 'Going Places' Literally." *Washington Post,* May 26, A15.

Orpilla, Mel. 2005. *Filipinos in Vallejo*. San Francisco: Arcadia.

Orrick, William H. 1969. *Shut It Down! A College in Crisis: San Francisco State College, October, 1968–April, 1969*. Report to the National Commission on the Causes and Prevention of Violence. Washington, D.C.: U.S. Government Printing Office.

Pido, Antonio J. A. 1997. "Dimensions of Pilipino Immigration." In Root, *Filipino American: Transformation and Identity*.

———. 1986 *The Pilipinos in America*. New York: Center for Migration Studies.

Portes, Alejandro, ed. 1996. *The New Second Generation*. New York: Russell Sage Foundation.

———. 1995. "Children of Immigrants: Segmented Assimilation and Its Determinants." In *The Economic Sociology of Immigration: Essays on Networks, Ethnicity, and Entrepreneurship*, ed. Portes. New York: Russell Sage Foundation.

Portes, Alejandro, and Ruben G. Rumbaut. 1990. *Immigrant American: A Portrait*. Berkeley: University of California Press.

Posadas, Barbara M. 1999. *The Filipino Americans*. Westport, Conn.: Greenwood.

Putnam, Robert D. 2000. *Bowling Alone*. New York: Simon and Schuster.

Quinsaat, Jesse, ed. 1976. *Letter in Exile: An Introductory Reader to the History of Pilipinos in America*. Los Angeles: University of California Asian American Studies Center.

Revilla, Linda A. 2003. *An Untold Triumph: The Story of the 1st and 2nd Filipino Infantry Regiments, U.S. Army*. In *Viewers Guide*.

Rimonte, Nilda. 1997. "Colonialism's Legacy." In Root, *Filipino Americans: Transformation and Identity*.

Root, Maria P. P., ed. 1997. *Filipino Americans: Transformation and Identity*. Thousand Oaks, Calif.: Sage.

Rumbaut, Ruben, and Kenji Ima. 1988. "The Adaptation of Southeast Asian Refugee Youth: A Comparative Study." Final report to the Office of Refugee Resettlement, U.S. Department of Human Services, Washington, D.C.

Santos, Bob. 2002. *Hum Bows, Not Hot Dogs*. Seattle: International Examiner Press.

Scharlin, Craig, and Lilia V. Villanueva. 1992. *Philip Vera Cruz: A Personal History of Filipino Immigrants and the Farmworkers Movement*. Los Angeles: University of California Labor Center, Institute of Industrial Relations, and University of California Asian American Studies Center.

Schneider, Barbara, and David Stevenson. 1999. *The Ambitious Generation: America's Teenagers, Motivated but Directionless*. New Haven, Conn.: Yale University Press.

Sison, Marites N. 2004. "Not 'For Hong Kong Only.'" *Filipinas* 13, no. 143 (March).

Smith, R. M. 1997. *Civic Ideals: Conflicting Visions of Citizenship in U.S. History*. New Haven, Conn.: Yale University Press.

Smith, Ralph E., ed. 1979. *The Subtle Revolution: Women at Work*. Washington, D.C.: The Urban Institute.

Storey, Moorfield, and Marcial P. Lichauco. 1926. *The Conquest of the Philippines by the United States, 1898–1925*. New York: Knickerbocker.

Strauss, William, and Neil Howe. 1991. *Generations: The History of America's Future, 1584 to 2069*. New York: Morrow.

Takaki, Ronald. 1979. *Iron Cages: Race and Culture in Nineteenth-century America*. New York: Knopf.

———. 1989. *Strangers from a Different Shore: A History of Asian Americans*. New York: Penguin.

Tamoria, Leonor. 2000. "Hawaii's Filipino Supreme Court Justices: High Court Slam Dunks." *Filipinas* 9, no. 98 (November).

Tienda, Marta. 2002. "Demography and the Social Contract." *Demography* 39, no. 4:587–616.

Tocqueville, Alexis de. 2000. *Democracy in America*. Trans. and ed. Harvey C. Mansfield and Delba Winthrop. Chicago: University of Chicago Press.

Twain, Mark. 1901. "Thirty Thousand Killed a Million." Previously unpublished essay. *Atlantic Monthly*, April 1992, 52–65.

Urban Associates. 1974. "A Study of Selected Socio-Economic Characteristics of Ethnic Minorities Based on the 1970 Census." In vol. 2: *Asian Americans*, HEW publication no. (OS) 75-121. Washington, D.C.: Department of Health, Education and Welfare.

Weber, Max. 1958. *The Protestant Ethic and the Spirit of Capitalism*. Trans. Talcott Parsons. New York: Charles Scribner's Sons.

Wong, Jade Snow. *Fifth Chinese Daughter*. New York: Harper, 1950.

Index

About the Author

Juanita Tamayo Lott trained as a social scientist at the University of Chicago and as a policy analyst in the San Francisco and Washington, D.C., metropolitan areas. She is author of *Asian Americans: From Racial Category to Multiple Identities*, and is a contributing editor to *The Asian American Almanac*. She has written on demographic shifts for general public and scholarly audiences since 1976.

human observation, intervention, and control. The power of faith reinforces connections between human beings in terms of the accountability of the individual to the group and to the gods. Public atonement for sins, restitution to society, forgiveness, and reconciliation were played out in Greek choruses and continue to be played out in the *mea culpa, mea culpa, mea maxima culpa* of the Confiteor that is recited by many Filipino Americans at Sunday mass. There was the biblical calling, and also the concept of noblesse oblige, for "to whom much is given, much is expected." Not only are individuals and groups of individuals bound to one another by blood lines, tribal ties, and mutual survival, they are bound also by a collective conscience reinforced via bonds of faith. They are stewards of the earth's bounty and witnesses to each other's words and actions.

The constant migration of capital, knowledge, beliefs, and people all over the world permeates, shifts, and perhaps even breaks down the boundaries of the world's nation-states. Are we moving away from being group members of nation-states to becoming individuals with many or no group memberships? The forces of unity and the endurance of equal individuals versus the forces of division and the conquest of stratified groups are in tension at the beginning of this twenty-first century at both national and international levels. Another relevant factor to consider, but beyond the scope of this book, are "market-dominant minorities" at the group and national level. According to Amy Chua, economic globalization in the information age has resulted in free markets concentrating disproportionate, often spectacular wealth in the hands of a resented ethnic minority such as the Chinese in Southeast Asia, Croatians in the former Yugoslavia, and whites in Latin America and South Africa (2003).

Yet many Americans, including Filipino Americans, hold on to the dream of Martin Luther King Jr. The phenomenon of various groups coexisting, living, and working alongside one another over the decades with children and grandchildren of every color of the rainbow, is one manifestation of the future destiny of multigenerational Americans. Several states, particularly those with large populations, are becoming nonmajority states. The United States continues to shift toward pluralism, particularly among its younger generations. Common destiny, emanating from common ground, shared principles, and shared values, reaffirms the connection from one generation to the next.

Younger Filipino Americans can use their substantive skills to play and work collaboratively with other Americans of Generation X, the millennial generation and the digital generation to lead the United States into a true Pax Americana. Throughout U.S. history, however, shared values have oftentimes given way to divisive values, with Manifest Destiny resurfacing in old and new forms. In the future tension between Manifest Destiny and common destiny, will the U.S. succumb to the Peter Principle or to the planned obsoles-